A
Cadre School Life
Six Chapters -

By Yang Jiang
Translated by Geremie Barmé

The first articulate account on a period of China's history that lives on for many as both dream and nightmare.

A Joint Publication

A Cadre School Life: Six Chapters

幹校六記
楊　絳著
白杰明譯

A Cadre School Life
Six Chapters

By Yang Jiang
Translated by Geremie Barmé
with the assistance of Bennett Lee

Joint Publishing Co.
Hongkong 1982

Joint Publishing Co. (Hongkong Branch)
9 Queen Victoria Street, Hongkong

© *Joint Publishing Co. (Hongkong Branch) 1982*
All rights reserved

First published September 1982

Printed in Hongkong by
Tai Hwa Wing Kee Printing Factory
173 Wo Yi Hot Road 1F, Kwai Chung, Hongkong

ISBN 962-04-0222-7

Contents

Introduction

A *Cadre School Life: Six Chapters* is the first articulate account of life in a cadre school — the reform camps established for intellectuals throughout China following Mao Zedong's 'May 7 Directive' of 1966. Within a few years over twenty million people, virtually all of China's professional and university-trained population, were in such schools. Yang Jiang, a professor emeritus of English, writer and translator was 'sent down' to the cadre school of the Chinese Academy of Social Sciences in 1970 at the age of sixty. She and her husband, Qian Zhongshu (Mocun), a respected writer and scholar, lived in different regiments of the same school for two years, far from their home in Beijing, their recently widowed daughter and their life and work of twenty years. After having survived the turbulence of war, civil strife and revolution, both of them thought their lives would end in the cheerless and spartan surroundings of a cadre school.

In 1949, neither Yang nor her husband accepted the generous offers that had been made to them to live and teach overseas. They saw their personal fate irrevocably linked with China, and it was as a member of the massive commune-country in the throes of turning against itself during the Cultural Revolution that Yang Jiang participated in political study, manual labour and the struggle to overcome 'bourgeois ideology'. She records her life in the cadre school lucidly, attempting neither to praise nor condemn, with no desire to theorize or declaim. Instead of detailing the words and deeds of others, she simply chronicles the lives of herself and her husband. The result, as one of China's foremost critics comments, is a book that 'pervades one with a sense of sorrow and loss; we lament as she does but do not feel dejected, we sense her indignation at being wronged but find in this no hate or reproach. Every word is eloquent in its sincerity and truthfulness.'*

The style of Yang Jiang's *A Cadre School Life: Six Chapters* is inspired by the mid-Qing 'connubial-biography' of Shen Fu, *Six Chapters on a Floating Life*, a work highly praised for its subtle and unaffected language as well as for its realism. Yang's book is as rare and exceptional a piece of writing now as Shen's work was when it appeared two centuries ago. Its honesty, humour and irony have no trace of the sensationalism, forced style or flowery language that mar most of contemporary Chinese writing. Yang is an author whose life spans China's feudal past and uncertain future, someone with the training and sensibilities of a traditional scholar and who has both the sympathies and insight of a citizen of revolutionary China.

Just as Shen Fu's *Six Chapters on a Floating Life* conveys a moving and vivid picture of life in the Qing dynasty, so Yang Jiang's six chapters describes a period of China's history that lives on for many as both dream and nightmare. *A Cadre School Life: Six Chapters* is one of the first books to fulfill the writer Ba Jin's hope for honest and personal writing about the Cultural Revolution:

---

* See *Dushu* (Reading) magazine, Beijing, September 1981, page 11, *"Ganxiao liu ji" duhou* (After Reading *A Cadre School Life: Six Chapters*) by Min Ze.

" 'Forget! Forget!' Go on, call as you will. But let me warn you that no one can forget those eleven harrowing years. Let our descendants draw their own conclusions about what happened, let them write the history of it all. There'll be no lack of people to do that. But why shouldn't we leave them some first-hand material to work with? Why shouldn't we leave them a truthful record of what happened to us? Must we force ourselves to forget the anguish and the wounds of the past so we can look to the future and move forward? And by forgetting these wounds let them fester in our souls?"*

July 1982,   Geremie Barme
Kyoto

---

* See *Jue buhui wang ji* (I'll Never Forget), No. 28 of Ba Jin's *Suixianglu* (Random Thoughts), Volume 1, Joint Publishing Co., Hong Kong, 1979.

Foreword

After reading the manuscript of my wife Yang Jiang's *A Cadre School Life: Six Chapters*, I had the feeling that she had left out a chapter, one that might be called 'Politics — Chapter on Shame.'

I say this because the main task of our Academy of Studies cadre school was to 'make politics', and weed out 'May 16th Elements'.* Political struggles and criticisms were like a fever that stayed with us for the two years we were in the countryside, overwhelming us from time to time and consuming our energies when the more practical work of growing food, building accomodation, moving house, and so forth, did not demand our attention.

In this book Yang Jiang has written a Chapter on Labour, a Chapter on Idleness, chapters on this and chapters on that, yet these are no more than a few deft stitches in the tapestry of the times, whimsical asides in what is a tale of epic proportions.

Now that it is all over, we should be able to see just what

* An underground political organisation named after the Communist Party's 1966 May 16th resolution on the 'Cultural Revolution'.

happened.   In the Cultural Revolution, as in all of the political movements that proceeded it, one can find three different types of people.   First, the hapless victims, the comrades who were falsely accused of crimes, then criticised and struggled.   If they wrote memoirs, they would probably include a 'Chapter on Being Wronged', or a 'Chapter on Indignation'.

The second consists of the broad masses of China.   In their recollections of that period there might be a 'Chapter on Remorse', recording their gullibility and readiness to believe all of the trumped up charges made against others, and their thoughtless complicity in the persecution of innocents. Some, myself included, would record our remorse for our lack of courage.   For it was people like me who, although aware of the injustices being perpetrated on those around us, were too cowardly to take a stand and speak out against what was happening.   Our only boldness was a lack of enthusiasm for the endless movements and struggles in which we participated.

The third group is made up of those who knew all too well that things had gone wrong, and that basic questions of principle had long ago been buried under mountains of confusion and deception.   In spite of this, however, they continued to play the role of the revolutionary, instigating witch-hunts and acts of violence, and setting themselves up as the sole arbiters of truth.   These people have the most reason to write a 'Chapter on Shame'.   But they have the shortest memory of all; to them remorse is an unwelcome emotion.   Of course, they may have unconsciously suppressed their sense of guilt.   Or, what is more probable, they honestly believe they have done nothing to be ashamed of.

An acute sense of shame can result in selective amnesia: no one wants to remember things that have caused him or her a loss of face or embarrassment.   It is not surprising then that uncomfortable memories can slip unnoticed from conscious recollection into oblivion.   A guilty conscience makes you guarded and circumspect; it can hinder a person's struggle for existence. Someone weighed down by contrition and remorse may hesitate to advance and so fall by the wayside for the rest of his life. It is quite natural then that feelings of shame and guilt should be discouraged rather than cultivated. The ancients knew the wisdom of this and did not include 'shame' in their list of the Seven Emotions of Man. In this day and age, too much dwelling on the past and morbid feelings of guilt can be positively detrimental; better to be free of such things, leaving oneself with a clear conscience and a happy heart.

Only four chapters of Shen Fu's *Six Chapters on a Floating Life** — a book, by the way, I have a particular dislike for — are still extant. Yang Jiang's *A Cadre School Life: Six Chapters*, on the other hand, is lacking a chapter. One of the true growth industries of the modern age is the field of literary research in which collectors, art dealers and academics combine their efforts to discover previously unknown and often highly dubious manuscripts, which they then blithely attribute to the pens of both famous and unknown writers. Perhaps one day someone will 'unearth' the incomplete portions of both Shen Fu and Yang Jiang's works. Thus, swelled to full size, these two books may in their own small way make up for some of the deficiencies of this world.

Qian Zhongshu (Mocun)

December, 1980

---

* A poetic chronical in six chapters of married life by a merchant written in the 18th century.

Going Down
Chapter on Separation

We both worked in the 'Academy of Studies' — that is what everyone calls the Chinese Academy of Social Sciences — formerly the School of Philosophical and Social Studies of the Chinese Academy of Science. My husband, Mocun, was in the Institute of Literature, and I was in the Institute of Foreign Literature.

In 1969 all of the research personnel in the Academy were undergoing political reeducation under the direction of the Workers' and Liberation Army Mao Zedong Thought Propaganda Team. During the first phase of this process we were all ordered to move into our respective office buildings and to turn them into dormitories. Six or seven, sometimes as many as ten, people lived in each room. The day would begin with communal exercises out in the open, followed by group political study sessions that ran through the morning, afternoon, and went on even after dinner. This type of intensive ideological reform went on for a time, and then it was decided to let the older and more sickly intellectuals live at home; political study was cut down so that we only had sessions in the morning and afternoon. Both Mocun and I were allowed to move back home because of our age, yet we sensed, however, that our time together was limited and that it wouldn't be long before we were 'sent down' to a cadre school. The rumours that had been circulating in the Academy finally pinpointed the location of the school, but the date of our departure was still a matter of conjecture, so we had no choice but to wait.

Every day we would line up for our midday meal in our respective institute canteens. You could never get out of the line with a meal in anything under half an hour, and it was too much trouble to go all the way home to make something yourself. Besides, there was not enough time between political meetings to do so. The Propaganda Team gradually relaxed its supervision a little, and we were able to meet for meals outside. There wasn't much to eat in the restaurants either, and you still had to queue up for everything, but at least we were together and could talk to each other while we waited.

On the 3rd of November I was standing at the bus stop outside the main entrance of the Academy when Mocun came along in a crowd of people. He walked over, stood beside me and whispered,

"I've got something important to tell you, but wait until we're on the bus."

I studied his expression but couldn't guess what it was. After we had pushed and shoved our way onto the bus he finally said,

"I've been put in the advance party that's being sent down on the 11th."

Even though I had been preparing myself for this news, it still came as a great shock. The 11th was only a few days away, and we had wanted to celebrate his birthday together. We had been planning to have a special meal of *shou* noodles as it was Mocun's sixtieth 'empty year' birthday.* After

---

* *Shou* or longevity noodles are eaten on birthdays. 'Empty year' refers to the Chinese practice of calculating a child to be one year old at birth.

all, we said to each other, the way things were going it was not likely that we would be around to have the noodles on the proper occasion — our seventieth birthdays. Now even our hope of spending this day together had been shattered.

"Why have you been put in the advance party?"

"Because of you. Everyone else is going to be busy getting their families ready to go with them or making other arrangements for them, but they think I should be able to leave everything to you."

Their cadre school was located at Luoshan in southern Henan Province. The whole Institute was being sent down on November the 17th, about a week after the advance party set out.

We went to our usual restaurant and had a chicken hot-pot. The chicken was only bits of skin and bone, that added to the news I'd just heard, took my appetite right away, and even with the help of some soup from the hot-pot I couldn't manage to finish my rice.

Although there was only a week in which to get Mocun packed up and ready to go, they did not give him any time off from the Academy until two days before he left. I was able to take some time off so that I could help him prepare. Unlike previous stays in the countryside, this time everyone had been instructed to take all of their possessions; it seemed that in transplanting whole families this way, none of us was supposed to come back.

Everything he owned had to be bundled up and taken, including the things that he virtually never used: clothes that had been lying unworn in drawers, all of his books, notes, and so on. It made a surprisingly large pile of luggage. As both my daughter, Ayuan, and her husband, Deyi, had been sent to work in factories, they could only get away on their day off. They were a great help and used the now popular technique of tying up all of the luggage tightly with thick rope to protect it on its rough-and-tumble passage to the country. Heavy rope bindings could keep wood and steel trunks together well enough, but I came to learn that people are the most durable of all. Durability, being able to endure, is, I suppose, what 'being tempered' is really all about. In the end, all you really had to do was to prepare yourself for what was coming.

If the clothing he took with him was too old then it would never last; if it was too coarse then it would be difficult for him to wash. I had not done any mending for some time, but I took out the sewing machine and made a pair of coveralls for him out of the leftover material I had. Mocun could wear them for a long time without having to bother about washing. I also mended a pair of his old pants and stitched a large patch on the seat so that it looked like a flattened picture of the earth sewn together by cotton lines of longitude and latitude. It was as thick as cow-hide, but he seemed very happy and remarked that now he had a built-in seat so that he could sit down anywhere without worrying about getting dirty. He told me there was no need to get everything ready all at once since I would be able to take care of the rest when I was sent down. As for the children, he thought they could come and take care of both of us after they were posted to the countryside, too.

In no time at all the 11th arrived. Ayuan, Deyi and I went to the station to see him off. He was not travelling with very much hand luggage, so we found ourselves a corner in the waiting room to rest. It was a scene of utter confusion, with people in the advance party rushing around, all looking like they needed a few extra pairs of hands. Families and friends called each other, adding to the general chaos. Deyi immediately put down the things he was carrying and went to give some people a helping hand. Mocun and I looked on approvingly. We commented that the spirit of helping people in distress was something the new society really had taught the young. It was also a relief to know that our daughter was in the care of such a gentle and considerate young man.

As Deyi was still busy lifting and carrying other people's belongings, Ayuan and I helped Mocun with his things. After squeezing our way onto the platform, we hustled him onto the train to find a seat. Once he was settled in, the three of us went back out onto the platform and waited silently for the train to leave.

I remember how people seeing friends off on ocean voyages in the past used to throw coloured streamers on to the deck. There would be cheers and applause when the wispy paper lines snapped as the boat moved slowly away from the dock. There were usually tears among the happy shouts of well-wishing and farewell, as if the broken streamers had somehow torn the travellers and their loved ones apart. Although there were no streamers at the train station, there was an almost visible knot between the families and couples that were saying goodbye; but unlike those fragile strips of coloured paper, the poignancy of this farewell would not snap and flutter away when the train finally moved off.

After some time, Mocun walked back to the train door and told us not to wait any longer. We stood there looking at each other for a moment; there was nothing more to say. I decided it was better for the three of us to go rather than wait and let him see how worried we were that he was leaving alone. As we walked away, I could not help looking back after every few steps: the train still had not moved and people were milling around on the platform. We went home in silence. Ayuan and Deyi headed back to factories that they had been sent to by their university.

A few days later, someone from the Institute of Literature told me that Mocun's group could have their own beds shipped down to the cadre school provided they were tied securely with rope and sent to the Academy immediately. I set to work at once. It wasn't long before I found out that there was a knack to making stiff thick rope stay in one place once you have something tied up. The secret lies in what you do with the ends — whatever you do you shouldn't tie a knot; you have to stuff the ends under the rest of the rope so they will not slip out. I also soon realized that you need at least two people to 'draw and quarter' a normal size bed but, since I was by myself and only had a day to get it done, I forged on regardless.

Once the small wooden bed of ours was dismantled, however, no matter how I juggled the individual pieces, I just couldn't strap them together in one parcel. By this time I regretted that I had not been blessed with an extra arm, my teeth being the only unoccupied part of my anatomy with which I could hold the loose end of the rope steady. Finally, out of sheer frustration, I decided to separate the pieces into a few bundles. To make things more manageable I added a length of string to the end of the rope and tied up the dismembered bed in three sections. On each section I wrote Mocun's name a couple of times. It was only a bed but I worried over it as if it were a family of refugees, and I fretted that once the pieces were separated they would never find their way back together again. At last I sent it off. From the letter I later got from Mocun I gathered he had as much trouble locating those three parcels as I'd had in tying them up.

— The Institute of Literature and another institute were sent down first. As military vocabulary was then in vogue no one called them institutes, but rather 'regiments'. On the day that these two regiments were officially sent down we were all given a 'free day' to go and cheer them off on their trek. They had all lined up in ranks and marched past us to the sound of cymbals and drums, proceeded by a large red flag. Our old colleague and mentor, Yu Pingbo, and his wife were at the head of the columns. Seeing this seventy year-old scholar lining up as though he was in kindergarten I felt sick at heart; I had seen enough and turned away. I was not the only one who lacked the required enthusiasm for the ceremony, and I noticed that a number of others were heading back to the offices as well.

All of us knew we were going to be sent down to be reformed, yet no one had the heart to reflect on the poignancy of separation from family and home as the literati of the past had done in their poetry and writing. Some sections of the Academy had already left and those of us who remained had to work harder than ever. We were made to do political study all day every day, so much so that even the 'worker teachers' assigned to reeducate us became bored. One of them, in his early twenties, grumbled, "Standing all day long in front of a blazing steel furnace never bothered me, but now my head aches, my back aches — all this sitting around is killing me." It seemed that tempering hardened intellectuals was far more demanding than tempering steel. Learning how to be occupied by doing nothing was also quite an art.

The key to our ideological reformation was participation in manual labour. After completing a network of underground air-raid shelters at the Academy, we began moving books. This consisted of bundling, tying and carrying heavy volumes from one building to another. Or, for a change, we would shift piles of books from one room to another. When we had finished relocating the books of our own institute, we set to work on the books of another institute. Once we were directed to clear out a one-room library smothered under years of dust and obvious neglect. Our job was to remove all of the books, book cases and shelves so that the room could be used for some other purpose. While we busied ourselves, anyone who walked into the room would nearly choke on all of the dust that we had stirred up, sneezing non-stop for several minutes. Although we all wore surgical masks we still ended up with dirty faces, coughing up black phlegm. The bitter cold of winter had given way to the heat of early summer, and the heavy work of carting steel book-cases and huge card-files — each brimming with now useless index cards — made us all break into a sweat. The heaviest work was left to the younger and more able-bodied of our group who carried everything out on their shoulders. The friction gradually wore through the material to the flesh underneath.   Flesh and bone were still the most durable.

The weaker ones always had it easier.   I only had to do a little light work—nothing to speak of really.   Whenever I had some free time I would make up a small package for Mocun and send it off to him at the cadre school.   He wrote to me every chance he had.   They were short sketchy letters, but he wrote every day.   Had I been able to save them, what interesting reading they would make today!   Then again, far more important and valuable letters were destroyed without a second thought, so this hardly seems important now.

When Mocun's group arrived at Luoshan they had to clean up an old labour reform camp barracks to live in.   The building, abandoned years ago, was covered in cobwebs and dirt.   The weather was already very hot, and though they had spent the first night sleeping on straw mats he said they were still sweltering.   But suddenly there was a freak snowfall and the weather turned bitterly cold again, the ground outside dissolving into slippery mud.   On the 17th the rest of the Institute arrived and the eighty 'bachelors' squeezed onto a long earthen *kang** under the same roof.   One fellow had taken his young son with him, a little devil who urinated all over the *kang* before going to sleep, 'fertilizing' the bed for his elders.   On their day off everyone went over to the nearby township to buy food.   Mocun told me that they had roast chicken and cooked tortoise on sale at the local market, but when I asked him what the tortoise tasted like, he wrote back that he had not eaten any.   He also sent me a few rough poems.

As there was no tillable land at Luoshan, none of them had anything to do, so after a month or so of complete

---

*   A long brick platform heated from below and commonly used as a bed in north China.

inactivity, all of the 'students' in the regiment packed up their belongings in cases and baskets and moved off to Dongyue in Xi County. I managed to find the county on the map, but Dongyue was too insignificant to be marked. It turned out to be a desolate and remote place where there was hardly enough kindling around to keep a fire going in the winter. Quite a number of women in the company developed chilblains on the face because of the cold. They had to wash clothes by pitching them into a pond before beating them clean. Mocun gave his new shirt to an old woman from the village to wash, but she took it away and he never saw it again. I was worried that he might lose his footing on the slippery edge of the pond if he tried to do his own washing, so losing the occasional piece of clothing in this way was not too great a price to pay for his safety.

All the people in Beijing who were waiting to be sent down were anxious to hear about conditions in the cadre school, so I was being asked constantly for the latest news from Mocun. Among the more factual pieces of information were a few anecdotes, the most popular one being about the poet He Qifang and the fish. The cooks in the mess decided to treat everyone to a meal of red-fried fish freshly caught from the newly-drained marsh. On hearing the news, Qifang grabbed the mug in which he kept his toiletries and went to buy himself a serving of fish. As he was eating he noticed that it had rather a strange flavour. Finally, after a few more mouthfuls, he used his spoon to dredge the largest piece out of the bottom of the mug to make a closer inspection. Only then did he realize he had been eating fish seasoned with an old piece of soap that had stuck to the bottom of his mug. When I told everyone this story they burst out laughing, but it was a laughter softened by a feeling of sympathy for the old man. They in turn told me an anecdote they had heard about Mocun. He and a friend called Ding apparently had sat together for hours nursing a pot of water while waiting for it to boil. When all my colleagues started laughing I became a little defensive and tried to explain that the stove was a very slipshod affair that had been built outside and was exposed to the wind and snow, so naturally it was difficult to get a pot of water to boil. Nevertheless, a joke is a joke and everyone giggled on merrily despite my explanation.

After Chinese New Year, they started building themselves some new housing. The women pulled carts of mud, made bricks and laid them just as the men did. Mocun, Yu Pingbo and a few other 'old, weak, ill and disabled' members of the regiment were excused from this heavy labour, but helped out anyway doing odd jobs and some light work. After they had been out there for eight months, our regiment was finally sent down to join them. By that time they were already settled in barracks which they had built themselves.

Our regiment set out on the 12th of July, 1970. When Mocun had left Beijing, Ayuan and Deyi had come along to the station to see him off. Now that I was going, Ayuan was the only one left to come and say goodbye. Deyi had killed himself a few weeks earlier.

Deyi had never made a secret of the fact that he was 'a little to the right' in his attitude to the Cultural Revolution; he said he just could not accept the way the ultra-leftists were carrying on. When the purge of 'May 16th activists' began, a few extreme leftists who were suspected of belonging to the banned organisation 'confessed' that Deyi was the head of their cell, and that he was in possession of a full name list of the other members. Having already finished his stint of labour in the factory, Deyi had meanwhile returned to the university. Ayuan was still at her factory, and as they had different days of the week off they were never home at the same time. The last time he went back to school he said to me,

"I can't let them accuse me of refusing to cooperate with the revolutionary masses, but what chance do I have of standing up to the Propaganda Team? The only alternative is to make up a list of names and get a lot of other people into trouble. But I've never been a convincing liar."

As soon as he got back to the university, he was detained. Class struggle had enveloped everything and Ayuan was ordered back to the university immediately along with all of the other students who were still working in factories. The Workers' Propaganda Team took charge of Deyi's case, and arranged for everyone in the department to 'struggle' him. They wanted to pressure him into producing a list of names. Instead he committed suicide.

Once I had settled into the carriage, I went out just like Mocun had and told Ayuan not to wait for me any longer. I knew very well that she was not a helpless child and that I could leave her to fend for herself without worrying, but as I watched that listless, solitary figure walk away from me, I felt as though I was abandoning her. I forced myself to shut my eyes, but in the darkness I could see her even more clearly — returning alone to that disordered, comfortless place that used to be our home, and cleaning up after my final rushed packing. As I could not bear the thought of this, I opened my eyes wide again, but she was already gone. I shut them once more and let the tears flow down into my heart. The train slowly creaked into motion and I left Beijing.

———————

Mocun was so dark and thin that he looked like a complete stranger. But no matter how much his appearance had changed, I recognized him in an instant.

There was a doctor by the name of Huang in the school clinic who was known for being very frank and stubborn. Once when Mocun had gone for an appointment, she had glanced at the name in the register and exclaimed,

"What? You're not Qian Zhongshu. You can't fool me, I know the man."

Mocun stood his ground and refused to be intimidated. Doctor Huang was adamant,

"I know his wife, too."

Refusing to be put off, Mocun told her my name to prove that he was my husband.   To spare herself any further argument she dropped the matter, though she wasn't really convinced that he was not an imposter.   When I mentioned the incident to her later she burst out laughing,

"Well, you can hardly blame me, can you?   He doesn't look anything like he used to."

I cannot remember now just what he did look like at the time, or even what he was wearing; my attention was rivetted by an ugly red pimple on his jaw.   Although no larger than a hazel-nut, it had a nasty head on it and looked very angry. The tip of the head was a bright red surrounded by dull yellow pus.   It was the first thing I noticed when we met again, and I remember saying,

"That's a very bad ulcer.   We'll have to get a hot compress on it at once."

If it had not been for me who would have given a thought to treating it with a hot compress?   I looked through their Red Cross medicine chest and discovered they had gauze and absorbent cotton, but there wasn't a scrap that had not been dirtied by careless muddy hands.

Mocun told me that this was his second ulcer.   After the first one had come up, the leadership had given him a few days rest and moved him away from the boiler where he had been working.   By the time we met he had been allocated new duties: he was in charge of the tools during the day and was on duty at night as a watchman.   His immediate superior had given him half a day's leave in honour of my visit, but my brigade leader was not so lenient, and I was only permitted to make a short visit to Mocun's regiment with someone from my brigade who had some business there; I was expected to return almost immediately.   Mocun walked back to my regiment with me, and we parted again, hardly having time to say anything to each other. Ayuan and I still had not told him about Deyi's death, and it was hardly the appropriate time to tell him then and there. I got a letter from him two days later and he told me that the pimple was an ulcer, just as I had said, and that after it had been lanced they had given him a few injections and it was starting to go down.

Even though we only lived an hour away from each other we were at the command of our respective leaders and had to 'follow orders and obey the rules'. Not being free to do what we liked, we continued to communicate by letter, though they did let us see each other on our days off. This 'day of rest', though not on a Sunday, only came once every ten days, so we all called it 'the big Sunday'. If the leadership decided there was something more important to do on the day then the holiday was cancelled. Despite everything, however, we were more or less together, unlike Ayuan, who was all alone in Beijing.

Well Digging
Chapter on Labour

There was always lots of work to be done in a cadre school. Labour out in the fields consisted mainly of planting beans or wheat. In the hot weather this meant that the day would start in the early hours around three when everyone would set off to work on an empty stomach. Breakfast would be brought out to you at six, then work continued until midday before you headed back for lunch. Following the afternoon rest, you would return to the fields around dusk and work into the night.

At the beginning we stayed in the peasants' houses in the village, but work started on our own accomodation almost at once. As bricks were unavailable we had to make our own mud substitute. Brick-making was regarded as the most backbreaking work. Looking after the pigsties and tending the pigs ran a close second, since it was the dirtiest and most unrewarding job of all. Most of the older and less robust 'students' such as myself were assigned to the vegetable gardens and kitchens, all of the heavy and tiring work falling on the shoulders of the young.

One night there was an evening of performances and skits on the theme of manual labour. Among the sketches was a short play about a member of a certain regiment who risked life and limb to keep the fire in a brick kiln going even though the roof was about to cave in. Someone said it was based on a true story. Another regiment put on a performance that was simply called 'Well-digging'. The whole regiment crowded on to the stage and moved around in a large circle as though they were pushing a well drill while they chanted a work song in chorus. There was no script and no other action apart from the circling movement and rhythmic chanting. Everyone moved and worked as one, drilling on without stopping until they reached the right depth. 'Hey-ho, hey-ho!' — the choral reverberation reminded me of a once-popular film theme song, 'The Song of the Volga Boatmen'. Listening to the performers, I could nearly see the boatmen on the riverbank pulling their boats along, step by step, struggling forward exhausted and leaning all of their weight against the ropes. Although the well-digging piece was a little monotonous it was more realistic and moving than the heroics in the kiln with its message 'to fear neither hardship nor death.' At the end of the evening everyone went away full of praise for the well-digging performance; after all, people said, it didn't require any rehearsal: all they had to do was climb on the stage and do it.

Suddenly someone blurted out,

"Just a minute. There must be something ideologically wrong with it . . . It must be . . . that is, if intellectuals are so impressed by it, it must mean . . . "

Everyone understood the point he was trying to make and laughed knowingly. This was followed by an uncomfortable silence. We quickly changed the subject.

———————

I was assigned to work in the vegetable brigade. One of our major tasks was the digging of our own well, just like those people on stage, and we did it without any machinery.

The district in which our cadre school was located had

had a run of good luck—although it was right next to the flood-prone Huai River, the area had not been washed out for a good two years. On the other hand, the ground was bone-dry and hard as rock, and this made growing vegetables quite a chore. The local peasants had a saying: "It's muddy when it rains and like rock when it's clear." A tractor had gone over the ground before we went to work on it, but all the plough had done was turn up great sods of earth as big and as hard as small boulders, so we still had to put a lot of work into just getting the ground really to plant. Breaking up those sods into workable earth was not only exhausting, but it required the patience of a saint as well. Once we had finally carved out a few patches of earth and dug out water channels, we discovered that there was no water on hand. In a neighbouring vegetable garden there was a motor-pump well that supposedly went to a depth of ten metres. We were constantly going over to get drinking water from them. The water in a hand-dug well of about three metres' depth was always muddy. To obtain drinkable water from it you had to put disinfectant in the bucket, which always made the water taste very peculiar. But the water from the motor-pump well, ten metres down in the earth, was cool and sweet. Drinking that water after sweating in the sun for hours was like sipping nectar.

Our borrowing was not limited to a neighbourly cup or two of drinking water, since we always took the liberty of washing our dirty hands and feet, too. None of this caused any trouble, but when we tried to use the well to water our vegetables there were numerous problems. For one thing, without a pump we couldn't get any water over to our fields. Once we managed to borrow a pump, but the water from their well had barely started its torturous route through our carefully dug system of channels — wasting most of itself in the dry earth on the way — when it got dark and the people we borrowed the pump from came to take it back. The spinach seeds we had planted took a whole month to sprout, and then did so only after a heavy rainfall. In the end we decided that we would have to dig our own well. After selecting a site we all set to work.

The designated ground was as hard as burnished copper. I picked up a shovel and stabbed down with what I thought was enough strength to gouge out a great hole in the ground, but only managed to make a white scratch on the surface, much to the amusement of the younger people around me. But when even their more energetic efforts were not getting them very far they agreed it was a job for pickaxes. Although I wasn't very good with a shovel, I was pretty fast on my feet, so I volunteered to run over to the tool shed to get them. Before long I was jogging back with the picks over my shoulder to find the others still chipping away at the ground. As soon as I appeared a couple of the young men took the picks from me and began loosening the earth with them. The stronger men worked with the picks in turn while the rest of us shovelled the earth out of the way. We kept at it all day and by dusk had managed to scoop out a fair-sized hole, but there still wasn't a hint of moisture at the bottom of it. One of the younger members of the group, Xiao Niu, began grumbling about women being bad luck and how they were unlikely to find water with us around. There were only two women in the vegetable brigade: myself, the oldest woman in the whole company, and Axiang, the youngest, an overseas Chinese girl barely half my age. Xiao Niu's loud comments came as a shock to her and she couldn't make up her mind whether to be angry or amused. Finally, with a grin she told me she was determined to give him a piece of her mind. In all honesty, however, we were both a little worried that if we didn't find water very soon, everyone *would* blame us. Fortunately, the ground became soggy and then water began appearing at about a two-metre depth.

Shovelling out dry earth had been tiring enough, but scooping the heavy mud from the bottom of the well proved to be even more exhausting. Two people stayed down at the

bottom of the well and passed the mud up in buckets to
be dumped to the side by those standing at the rim. It
didn't take long before the ground around the well was
muddy, and everyone was slipping around in bare feet.
Axiang seemed to be enjoying herself the most and, having
taken off her shoes, had jumped into the well to help pass
up buckets of mud. I wasn't strong enough to lift even
one of the buckets, but joined in the spirit of things by
shovelling the mud around the well into a pile in my bare
feet.

The distaste one has for mud — with its usual mixture of
phlegm, mucus, urine and faeces* — vanished once we had
taken off our shoes and socks and started walking around in
the warm and yielding ooze. It was slippery and wet, but it
did not seem at all 'dirty'. You felt the way you did about a
loved one with a contagious disease, holding hands and
kissing without concern for becoming ill yourself. The
thought suddenly struck me: is this what they mean about
'changing your attitude' toward physical labour?

The digging became harder as water collected in the
bottom of the well. Though it was not like using a mechanical
drill where you have to keep on digging until you reach the
proper depth no matter how long it takes, still we could not
afford to slacken our efforts. We decided to follow the same
routine as the people planting crops, assembling in the
vegetable garden every morning before dawn without eating
breakfast. As the time for the morning meal approached,
Axiang and I would go back to get steamed bread, rice
porridge, salted vegetables and boiled water, load it onto a
wheelbarrow and cart it back to the well-site. I would push
it on the level and downward sloping parts of the dirt path;
Axiang would take over on the sharp turns, bumps and

---

* Urban Chinese regard walking barefoot as distasteful and mud with absolute
revulsion.

inclines. Although it doesn't sound like a very hard job, it took some practice to keep that cart on an even keel and the open tureens of porridge and hot water from spilling. I tried doing Axiang's job and quickly found that it looked much easier than it was. Luckily for me she didn't begrudge having to do the more difficult work and we got on very well together.

At lunchtime, everyone went back to eat at the regimental mess, and after a midday sleep continued working until dusk. We were always the last ones to get back for dinner. I don't remember how long we kept this routine up, but eventually we hit the three-metre mark. A few days before this the water at the bottom of the well was slowing work up so much that we had to ask a couple of strong young men from other units to lend us a hand. They jumped down into the well and set to work immediately in ankle-deep water. Wells are usually dug in the winter when the earth below is warm, but it was the height of summer and the well was damp and chilly. Axiang and I were afraid they would get a bad chill if they stayed down there too long, but they shouted back that they felt fine and kept on digging. We didn't want to seem like a pair of old hens, but we couldn't help going over to the well every so often to see how they were getting along.

The water gradually rose to knee level. After a while the diggers were splashing up to their thighs and then up to their waists. We had calculated that a three-metre depth would be quite sufficient for our purposes, so when they neared the mark I suggested that I go and buy some wine to warm the men who had been working in the water and to celebrate the completion of the well. After all the work we had put into it everyone was very excited. One of the men who had come over to help us dig was in charge of the rear-services unit. He gave me a few pointers on how I could get some wine. I rushed back to the regiment mess hall to recite to the cook what I had been told and got a bottle from him. On it was a threatening label with a skull and crossbones crudely drawn over the word *POISON*, which was followed by three large exclamation marks — obviously scribbled on to keep others from stealing it.   Protectively clasping the bottle, which still had about an inch of wine left in the bottom, I hurried off to the supply store at the central headquarters of the school, about one kilometre west of the vegetable garden.   I went as quickly as I could as I was worried about making it before closing time and wished I had one of those old flying-horse talismans tied to my feet so that I could go even faster.   But when I got to the store and found they were still open, I still had to talk them into selling me wine without an official authorisation form.   Luckily, the fact that I had managed to get hold of a wine bottle seemed to be official enough for them and they sold me a catty of rice spirits with no further questions asked.   They didn't have anything on sale to go with the wine so I had to settle for some 'sweets' that looked more like hard lumps of mud than anything else.   Then it was back to the well-site with my precious cargo.

They had finished the digging and everyone was sitting down for a rest.   As soon as they saw me, they all grabbed their drinking mugs and hurried over to pour themselves some wine.   We managed to finish the whole bottle I had bought, leaving only an inch or so at the bottom to be returned to the mess.   The 'sweets' also disappeared and our victory banquet drew to a close.

I had only been doing light work cleaning up around the construction site, and I can't say I personally experienced the tremendous physical exhaustion of well-digging, but at the end of every day I would lie awake listening to my companion tossing and turning in the next bed, moaning in her sleep as though struggling to tear herself away from the aches and pains of the day's toil.   I listened with a sense of guilt, knowing I was not really sharing the full burden of fatigue with her.   During the day as we were working, you even heard the men say, "Ah, I suppose we're not as young as we used to be," admitting that they no longer had the strength and energy of their early twenties. So even the people who were so much younger than me seemed to feel that they couldn't do as much as they would have liked to.

By the time we bought and installed a hand-driven pump, the well was full. We placed a platform over the top of the well with the pump positioned in the centre, so that a long handle was required to turn it. The advantage of this was that you didn't get dizzy pushing the handle since you had to walk in a large circle. The younger men in the brigade took turns at pumping water, doing from a few dozen to a hundred revolutions in one go. The people who sometimes came over to give our brigade a hand with the vegetables were impressed. They had realized that it took some time to get used to long periods of squatting when working in a vegetable patch, but not that turning a hand pump was also an acquired skill.

I was truly part of the team, going out with everyone else before dawn and returning to base camp only after dark. Though you couldn't say what I did was manual labour in the strict sense of the word, just being with everyone else and doing light jobs around the site made me feel part of it all. I gradually developed a sense of group or team spirit, a fellowship in which I was part of the whole. There was a satisfying feeling of belonging. I had never had this feeling when I had worked on short term community labour projects in the past; with those, once the assigned work or construction job was completed, everyone had gone their separate ways. Intellectual work is even less conducive to a team spirit. Even when you collaborate with other people, you tend to regard your own individual contribution as the most important. If you write an article with someone else, the person in charge of collecting and collating material and the person who actually writes it up very rarely manage to work as one. In the cadre school it was different: the prospect of an indefinite future of working together with little or no hope of ever going back brought about a strong feeling of community, of 'us-ness'.

I often heard people who had been sent down to the cadre school comment, "Well *they* never get soaked in the rain or sunburnt from working outside." A few simple words would carve a chasm between 'them' and 'us'. Being part of the 'us' by no means meant that we thought and acted as one: although we were now all in the same cadre school together, some had come down after being locked up in the 'cowshed'.* Despite these differences we were all part of the same category because we were all under 'them'. But you couldn't say that all of the people in charge of us were equally part of 'them', since *they* were only the ones who 'never got soaked in the rain or sunburnt'. I remember one person who really thought of himself as something special, giving orders and lecturing people in liberal fashion. He was a typical one of 'them'. Then there were others like 'that thick-skinned old fart', or 'the joker who thinks he's God's gift to mankind', — without a doubt also part of 'them'. The difference between 'us' and 'them' really had little to do with political or social class, yet working in a group all the time did give me much insight into the nature of 'class feelings'.

The poor and lower-middle peasants — the people we were all supposed to regard as our teachers, the people we had in fact been sent to the countryside to learn from and be reeducated by — actually took exception to our presence. One morning we arrived at our vegetable garden to discover that a number of rows of sweet potatoes had disappeared during the night. I lost count of the number of times vegetables we had planted were stolen before that had grown to full size. If you said anything, they'd protest loudly,

* Intellectuals were generally referred to as 'cow spirits and snake demons' in the Cultural Revolution, and the temporary prisons for confining them between struggle sessions became known as 'cowsheds'.

"Look at you, you buy all of the vegetables you eat anyway. You're only planting these for fun!" They also took all of the saplings we had planted and sold them at the local market. When we were harvesting our soya beans they relieved us of the rest of the crop before we had even finished. To add insult to injury, they would shout out in self-defence, "You people eat grain you've bought from the State anyway."

We were never part of their 'us', but only another type of 'them', or, as they put it, 'well-fed, wrist-watch-wearing oddities who like to dress up in old clothes.'

The Vegetable Garden
Chapter on Idleness

Everyone in our regiment put all they had into their work and did their best to eat as much as they could at each meal. I suppose you could see this as being a new application of the socialist principle of 'from each according to his ability and to each according to his needs'. That is putting it too simply since everyone was still receiving their former wages, which weren't based on the actual needs of the individual in the first place.

I never ate very much, and, because I was weak, didn't do any heavy work, but my old salary remained unchanged. As I was getting much more than most of the others, you could say I was really profiting from 'the superior system of socialism', or more crudely, that I was living off the fat of the land. I wasn't happy with the situation, but since no one appreciated the guilt and embarrassment I felt, I had no choice but to keep quiet and take care of my vegetables as well as I knew how.

There is always a lot to be done in a new vegetable plot. The first priority is to build an outhouse. As well as providing for our own convenience, we hoped that an outhouse would entice passers-by to add to our stock of organic fertilizer. With this in mind we decided to build it by the main thoroughfare at the northern end of the vegetable garden. The structure was very basic — five wooden posts, one positioned at each corner of the enclosure and a fifth planted on one side to form an entrance. We made the walls out of straw, and inside we buried a large pot up to the rim for our catch. On either side of the pot we dug shallow trenches, placing a few bricks in them for foot-holds. When we had finished, Axiang and I decided to cover the gaping hole of the entrance with a curtain, so we stripped the hard outer layer off some straw and hand-wove the stalk onto lengths of thin rope. Before long we had a very presentable screen. After hanging it up on the entrance we felt quite proud of our achievement. But when we arrived at the vegetable garden the next morning, our new screen was nowhere to be seen. Moreover, the growing pile of human fertilizer had been spirited away as well. From then on whenever Axiang or I went to the toilet, the other would have to stand at the entrance and act as a human screen.

There were no fences around our vegetable garden and on three sides there were patches that belonged to other regiments in the school. In one of these 'brother patches', our neighbours had built themselves a very fancy toilet, the contents flowing into a pit to the side of it. The hole inside had been laboriously lined with bricks, but in spite of this their 'holdings' were often stolen because the peasants believed that the faeces from the cadre school were especially effective as a fertilizer.

We decided to dig a long shallow trench for a compost heap to increase our yield of fertilizer. When it was completed, everyone cut grass and weeds to mix with it, but while we were eating our lunch all of the green grass we had cut disappeared, probably winding up as feed for the peasants' stock. I suppose we really shouldn't have been surprised; there wasn't very much vegetation in the area and even dry grass was pulled up roots and all to be used as fuel.

The regiments that had been sent down before us had built quite a few brick huts in their vegetable gardens so they could keep guard over their crops. All we managed was a hastily erected thatched hut on the southwest corner of the well. First we set up a wooden frame and made a mud wall on the northern side; the other three sides were built of thatched straw. The roof was also constructed of thatch with a piece of oil-cloth on top and a layer of vinyl underneath. To the northwest of the garden was a brick kiln that also belonged to the Academy. We went up with our wheelbarrow and collected the broken bricks and shards lying around outside to lay on the floor of the hut so it wouldn't be too damp for whoever was on duty. On the southern face of the hut we left an opening for an entrance and put a wooden door there with a lock on it. The head of our brigade, the brigade poet and Xiao Niu moved into the new hut so there would be a twenty-four hour watch on the vegetables. The rest of us had a place where we could take a rest under cover during the daytime.

Bit by bit we planted vegetables in all of the fields. We mostly planted Chinese cabbage and radishes, but there were also a few rows of lettuce, chives, potherb mustard, asparagus lettuce, carrots, parsley and garlic shoots. About this time we moved into our new accomodations. Unlike the barracks of a few of the regiments which had been sent down before us, ours was near the school headquarters. As our regiment was also allocated a vegetable patch right next to the new barracks, all of the able-bodied men in our brigade were transferred there to dig trenches. Our main vegetable garden could not be left unattended, however, so Axiang and I stayed behind.

Our first job was to tie up with pieces of vine all of the cabbages that were growing loose-leafed. Some of them had leaves that still had not opened out, but as they were not growing tight to the centre of the plant we tied them up too.   Besides that, all of the plants needed nourishment. Axiang was strong enough to carry a half-full bucket of 'organic fertilizer' in each hand out to me in the field where I would feed the plants with a cup. The vegetables we gave our particular attention to were the long white radishes — our precious Ivory and Taihu varieties. They had just broken through the ground, about an inch tall and as big as the diameter of a small rice bowl. We congratulated ourselves for their growth and were excited that our toil had begun to show results. We were also proud that our radishes were the 'cream of the crop'. Our brigade leader told us that we could put the plant ash that had been set aside for the carrots on our radishes. When it came time to harvest, I went over to the field thinking that I would be pulling up radishes at least six inches to a foot long, but when I bent over and gave the first plant a mighty tug, the earth gave way easily and I fell backwards onto my behind tightly clutching a tiny radish with a few spindly roots. At the end of the day we had what must have been the largest crop of pigmy radishes in the history of farming. Some of the carrots were a little more substantial, though most of them were about the size of small pears.

With the coming of the colder weather, you could feel the biting north wind as you squatted in the fields loosening the soil or pulling out weeds. It would cut through your clothing and chill you to the bone. The days grew shorter; and it was always pitch black by the time we got back to the regimental mess for dinner. In December we were moved to the new barracks over by headquarters, Axiang was transferred to a new vegetable garden nearby, and the three men who lived in the hut only came back at night, so I was left during the daytime to take care of things by myself.

Our brigade leader had let me stay on in charge of the old vegetable garden because it was only a ten-minute walk to Mocun's barracks up past the brick kiln. Mocun had been put in charge of the tools, and our brigade leader often had me go and borrow things, so this always meant a second trip, of course, as I had to return the tool to Mocun once we were finished with it. Everyone looked on with amusement when they spotted me scurrying happily back and forth from the tool shed. Mocun not only had to register the name of people who borrowed tools, but also took turns as a night watchman. His real job, however, was being the regiment's courier. Every afternoon he would go off to the post office to collect the daily papers, mail and packages, and distribute them to the regiment. Our vegetable garden was between his barracks and the post office, so he would follow the winding course of the stream that ran from the north past the garden. Sometimes he would take a longer route and pass through the garden to say hello. Everyone would stop work and chat with him, but he never dared stay too long and was sure not to take this 'long-cut' too often.

When Axiang was still working in the garden with me she often caught sight of him first and would give me a friendly nudge, saying: "Look who's coming to see you." Mocun was usually on his way back from picking up the mail and the three of us would go and sit by the stream for a while. By the time Axiang was transferred and I was left in the garden alone, the stream had dried up and he would come through the garden on his way to the post office instead of walking a semi-circle around the stream. We were together for a short time every day, and I am quite sure these tête-à-têtes in the vegetable patch were more enjoyable than the lovers' trysts in dainty flower gardens so often described in the old novels and operas.

Later Mocun discovered he could walk in a straight line from the garden and cross a stone bridge near the post office without having to worry about the stream at all. I would wait every afternoon for him to come ambling down from the kiln. If the weather was good we would sit on the bank of the irrigation canal south of the hut sunning ourselves. When he was running late he would only have time to exchange a few words, perhaps handing me a short letter he had written before rushing off. Quite often I would lock up the hut and walk down to the stream with him, then hurry back in time to see him head south and over the horizon until he disappeared from sight. On his way back he was always in a hurry to deliver the letters and papers back at his barracks so he wouldn't cross over the stream to see me again. I always saw him walking along and could say anything I had forgotten to tell him from my side of the stream.

The vegetable garden was the centre of my new world. To the south there was a hillock everyone called Tiger Mountain after the Peking opera,* which formed a line with the brick kiln and Mocun's barracks behind it in the north. To the west of Tiger Mountain were the headquarters, the centre of the cadre school, and our regiment's barracks was on the eastern side of the compound. One of the other regiments had built their mess hall at the foot of Tiger Mountain and I went to buy my lunch and dinner there every day. Close by over to the west was a group of houses where I often went to get boiled drinking water. A little way to the south was a small hut where a stove was kept going all the time, so during the day I'd occasionally go there for water as well. I had my own small stove, of course, which was made from three old bricks and fueled with the chaff and dry weeds which I managed to collect. Since it was open to the wind it was sometimes impossible to light. Due south from the vegetable garden was the post office where Mocun went to pick up the newspapers and mail every day. To the east past the stream were fields that stretched away as far as the eye could see, broken in a few places on the horizon by clumps of trees — that was where the neighbouring village was. The house where I'd been billeted when we first

---

* *Taking Tiger Mountain by Strategy* was one of the eight revolutionary model operas that were much vaunted during the Cultural Revolution.

went down was in a hamlet called Yang Village located still further east. From my vantage point I felt like a spider nestled in the middle of a web stretching out to the four corners of the world; my catch was not stray insects or chance visitors, but ephemeral sights and sounds, floating thoughts and lone reflections.

After an early breakfast I would start off to the vegetable garden by myself, and usually bumped into the three men who lived in the hut on their way to eat at the mess at headquarters. When I got to the garden the first thing I would do would be to go over to the hut, take out the key hidden in the straw next to the door and put my bowls and anything else I had brought with me inside. After locking the door I'd set out on my rounds. The ground in the eastern part of the garden was hard and sallow. Though it wasn't particularly suitable for growing anything, we had planted our crop of carrots there. Anything that did manage to grow was stolen before we had a chance to harvest it. The thieves would tear the carrots roughly from the ground, usually leaving a part of the carrot in the earth. I always made this carrot patch my first stop on early morning duty so that I could dig out the broken remains of the stolen carrots and wash them in the well for a snack later in the day. Then I'd head for the northern end of the garden where we had planted cabbages. As soon as any of the plants started filling out, someone was sure to sneak along and chop them off at the base, leaving the roots and the gleaming white wound of the base gaping dumbly up from the ground. Once I found a few fully-grown cabbages that had been cut off at the roots and just left standing there untouched. Thefts were so common that we finally decided to harvest what was left of the crops before the vegetables were fully-grown rather than wait until there was no more than a few cabbage roots left.

One day after returning from my rounds, I went out to the back of the hut and found three peasant women pulling out our Chinese lettuce. As soon as they caught sight of me they ran off, but they hadn't expected I'd chase after them. I was fast on my feet and was making ground on them when they threw the stolen vegetables out of their baskets. Having rid themselves of their haul they didn't have to worry about me catching them. In chasing after them I was only doing what was expected of me. Frankly, I wished they hadn't thrown the vegetables away. Had they only gone a little further and got away, they could at least have had a meal of fresh vegetables at home, instead of leaving the scattered lettuce, which was of no use to me.

They had probably been passing by when they saw our vegetables and decided to make a foray into the garden. Usually it was a teenage girl or a woman in her late forties leading a dozen or so children out to collect wild grass and kindling. They all wore clothes made from a patchwork of coloured scraps of cloth and carried wicker baskets hanging from one arm and a small hoe or scythe in the other hand. At every stop they would fan out in groups of twos and threes, and cut and gather everything in sight with mechanical precision, furtively stuffing the catch into their baskets. Their raids on the sapling nursery were also carried out with considerable forethought and expertise. At first they left the branches they had hacked from the trees in the nursery, and only later took them out in tied bundles and concealed them in a ditch by the road. As mealtime drew near, you could spot these teams of scavengers, weighed down with bundled lumps of kindling and grass tied to their backs and hidden treasures stashed in their baskets, regroup and straggle off home.

The more daring boys would go as far as uprooting whole saplings, tying them together and throwing them into the stream for safe-keeping until it was time for them to return to the village.

They also made quick work of the stray straw and chaff left lying around our hut; and it wasn't long before two of the wooden posts holding up the outhouse were also taken. In the end none were left. The thatched walls of both the toilet and the hut began to thin out visibly soon after we had finished building them. It got so that I wouldn't dare leave for the regiment mess at Tiger Mountain to buy my meal until I had made sure that these teams of well-laden foragers were well on their way home.

When the time came to harvest the vegetables the villagers came over to cut the cabbages in their field south of our garden. Their experienced hands did the work quickly and efficiently as our small brigade of old and feeble novices plodded along. It made for an exhausting day, cutting and pulling the cabbages out of the ground, piling them up so they could be weighed and the weights recorded, then loading them onto vehicles and transporting them to the mess hall at headquarters. The peasants finished well before dusk and left their field as clean as though it had been swept, whereas we were still working and our field was covered in stalks and scraps of cabbage leaves. An old woman came over and sat outside the hut with a little girl waiting for our team to stop work so that they could collect the pieces of cabbage leaf scattered in the rush to finish. The little girl ran over to the edge of the patch where our brigade was working and then scampered back to the old woman to report on our progress. When the old woman at last stood up and said that it was probably alright to collect scraps, the little girl replied that there was nothing left. When they spoke quickly in their local dialect I couldn't catch everything they said, but I did hear them mention 'pig feeding'. I heard her say, angrily: "Even the landlords used to let us clean up the fields when they'd finished."

When I moved a little closer and asked them what use cabbage scraps were to them, the girl's eyes lit up. She told me that they boiled the shredded outer leaves of the cabbage in water until they were soft, then poured in a thick batter and mixed it together. "It's delicious," she assured me.

I had seen the unappetizing dark brown lumps of steamed bread the local peasants ate, and suppose the batter she was talking about was the same colour. I never did find out whether the cabbage scraps and batter were as 'delicious' as the little girl claimed. The tasteless old cabbage and bitter radishes we ate at virtually every meal probably wasn't much better than what they had, but the flavour of the food they ate, which the girl had described with such relish was something we should have experienced but never did.

We did not manage to grow anything worth harvesting in our patch of swede turnips at all. The biggest ones were about the size of peaches, while the smallest were no bigger than apricots. I gathered a pile of them and was picking out the larger ones to send off to the cooks when I noticed the same old woman standing by watching me closely. She asked me how we would prepare them. I replied that they might make good preserves or might taste alright just boiled. "What if I keep the big ones and let you have the rest?" I suggested. She happily agreed, but moved quickly to pick the largest ones to put in her basket. I didn't make a fuss, but when she'd finished, I took a few handfuls out of her basket and replaced them with smaller ones. She didn't complain about this, but left quite satisfied. I feel a pang of guilt when I think about it even now, because in the end the cooks did not use any of the vegetables I had saved for them Then again, even if I had known the vegetables were going to be wasted I wouldn't have dared give her any more. You simply couldn't afford to set such a precedent.

When we were pulling out weeds some of the young girls from the village came to watch. We imitated their local accent and struck up conversations with them. I gave them some green seedlings and they helped us do the weeding. They called all males 'big men', and though none of them were old enough to be married — they were all about 12 or 13 — their parents had already chosen their future mates. One girl pointed to a friend who, she said, already had 'in-laws'. The girl in question blushed shyly and denied it, claiming that it was actually the girl who had been speaking who had the in-laws. Neither of them could read. The family I had been staying with was relatively well off — neither of their two ten year-old sons had to earn their pocket money by herding cows, and both of them were still going to school, though their eighteen-year-old sister was illiterate. Her parents had used a matchmaker to find a husband for her and she was engaged. The young man was a PLA soldier from a neighbouring village who was about the same age as she was. They had never met, and he wrote her a letter with a picture of himself inside; he only had a primary school education and had the solid honest look of a peasant. Her parents called me 'elder sister' because we had the same surname, and they asked me to write a reply to the boy from their daughter. I sat, pen in hand, staring at the paper in front of me for a long time before I was able to piece a letter together by asking for suggestions from every-one in the room. Her future husband had never seen her picture.

I was constantly amazed that the young boys in the village, all of them in their mid-teens, never seemed to have anything better to do than wander around with large wicker baskets tied to their backs, throwing into them whatever they laid their eyes on. Sometimes seven or eight of them would band together to hunt rabbits by beating the ground with sticks made from small stripped saplings, screaming and shouting all the while. Once, when a few of them came stomping into the vegetable garden making a great commotion, I rushed over to see what was going on. They told me they were after 'cats' — 'cat' being the word they used for rabbit. I had barely finished telling them that our vegetable garden didn't have any 'cats' in it when a rabbit that had been hiding under a leafy vegetable nearby suddenly sprinted for safety. It was so fast that they had to send their dogs to hunt it down. For a few moments, there was some furious running and dodging before the rabbit was cornered by the four yelping animals. After a final, desperate leap into the air it fell to the ground and was savaged. When it pounced into the air my heart seemed to jump into my throat in sympathy. From that time on I never had the slightest interest in watching the hunt when I heard the boys screaming and beating their sticks.

One day — it was the 3rd of January 1970, I remember — at about three in the afternoon, two men suddenly appeared in the vegetable garden, and pointing over to the two grave mounds just beyond the southeast corner of the garden, asked me if they belonged to the cadre school. They'd heard that one of the tractor drivers who had been sent down to help set up the school overturned his tractor on a bridge and had drowned in the river. They wanted to know where he had been buried. I pointed to a spot much further away and told them that the tractor driver's grave was there. They hadn't been gone long when I noticed a few people digging on the bank of the stream just east of the carrot patch. There was a utility truck parked near them with a mat covering the back of it. I realised suddenly that they were going to bury someone, and that the men standing at the side in army uniforms were from the PLA Propaganda Team.

From where I was standing I could just make out that there were three or four people digging very quickly. Soon one of them jumped into the hole and continued digging, and it was not long before all of them were down there shovelling out the loose earth. One of them suddenly came running towards me. I thought he probably wanted a drink of water, but it turned out that he had broken his shovel and wanted to borrow one from me. I went into the hut and got one for him.

No one from the village was around, and I was the only person who saw the grave-diggers frantically digging away in the ground. When they had dug so deep that I could only see their heads and shoulders above the ground, they stopped: the grave was deep enough. I watched on in silent horror as they went over to the truck and, from under the mat in the back, lowered a corpse into the pit and covered it with earth.

When the man who had borrowed the shovel came to return it, I asked him if the dead person had been a man or a woman and what the cause of death had been. He told me what regiment they were from and said they'd just buried a thirty-three-year-old man who had committed suicide.

Winter days were short and the half-light of dusk had surrounded them by the time they had packed up, got in the empty truck and driven away. The lonely vegetable fields lay bare, and I slowly walked over to where they had been working. There was a freshly-piled mound of earth on the bank of the stream, but no one would notice that it was a new grave.

When I saw Mocun the following day I told him to be careful not to step on the mound of earth by the stream on his way to the post office as it was a grave and the corpse wasn't in a coffin. He returned from the post office with a lot of news: he had found out the deceased's name, that he had a family and that they'd sent a pile of luggage back to his home that morning.

There was a fall of snow not long after and I was worried that the earth on the grave would subside and crack, and that the dogs might find the body. The earth sank down slightly, but did not crack open.

I kept a solitary watch over the vegetable garden throughout the winter, even waiting there in the dark as the sun came up, shooting the beautiful colours of the morning through the clouds in the east. Slowly, groups of peasants, young and old, would come trailing along from villages all around dressed in colourfully-patched clothes, splitting into smaller teams of twos and threes just near the garden, and disappearing from sight for the rest of the day. As the late afternoon sun hovered in the west, they would gradually regroup and return home with the day's prizes. I often stood in the doorway of the hut with my dinner from the canteen looking at the dapple glow of twilight melting into night, the early evening haze lying somnolently over the vast expanse of land that stretched out to touch the sky. While I slowly ate my meal, the garden would fall under a cloak of darkness. There wouldn't be a soul in sight, and not even a flicker of light from the houses in the distant village was visible. Once I had finished eating I'd go inside the hut, sometimes catching the sound of the playful scuffling of field mice in the thatched walls or the dead leaves on the trees outside rustling in the wind. After washing my metal bowls and spoon in well water, I would lock up and walk back to my dormitory alone.

———————

Everyone else was always busy, and I seemed to be the only one who didn't really have anything to do. So thorough was my idleness that I felt guilty and restless, even bored. Although I wasn't the Commander of the Guard of 800,000, I now understood Lu Zhishen's feeling of frustration at having to hide away as a Zen monk in a temple on Wutai Mountain.*

When we were all still living with billets I wasn't working with the women I was rooming with, so I didn't go back to the village with them in the evening. I came and went by myself, and I suppose I really preferred it that way. Anyway, I liked walking in the dark: if you used a flashlight you could only see the little patch of light in front of you and nothing else. If, on the other hand, you walked in the dark you could make out what was around you. Every evening I wended my way back to the village alone along a twisting and rocky path.

———————

* Lu Zhishen is one of the bawdy heroes of the classical novel *The Water Margin* (Shuihu Zhuan)

As I neared the houses I could see the lights in the house where I was staying flickering through the trees. There was only a bed in a room waiting for me, a rectangular board covered by a mosquito net. Although I was living there it was not my home. I often found myself thinking of a painting I had once seen of an old man with a bundle filled with all of his worldly belongings slung over his back, a walking stick in his hand, making his way along a small track at the foot of a slope which led to an open grave. I felt as though I was that old man.

In the New Year, at the beginning of April on the Qingming Festival Day, the cadre school moved to a new location in Minggang. Before going, our whole brigade assembled in the vegetable garden one last time to tear down everything that had been put up and pull out whatever could be moved. When we had finished, a tractor came and turned the ground over so that not a trace of the fields or trenches was left. As we were about to set out, Mocun and I sneaked back to have one last look: The hut, well-stand, irrigation ditches, fields — everything had disappeared. Even the flat mound of earth over on the bank of the stream had gone. All that was left was a large area of freshly turned soil.

Xiao Qu
Chapter on Affection

Our vegetable brigade poet found a puppy near the kiln and carried it to us in his arms. The poet's surname was Ou (區), and since people sometimes mispronounced it as 'Qu', Axiang decided to call the dog Xiao Qu or Little Qu. The poet's revenge was swift and clever: he was not so unimaginative as to suggest that the puppy be called 'Xiao Xiang' after her, but named it 'A-qu' as though it was one of Axiang's relatives. But since Xiao Qu was easier to say, that name stuck. Fortunately, no one outside our brigade ever knew that Xiao Qu had originally been 'Xiao Ou'.

Using leftover pieces of brick from the kiln we built a small kennel on the southern side of the hut overlooking the garden, and put some straw inside it for bedding. Even then it was a cold and comfortless little hutch. The vegetable fields were crisscrossed with irrigation canals, so when Xiao Qu first came she was constantly falling into the water and getting soaked. Before the weather had started getting cold I had stepped into one of the canals by accident and for the rest of the day squelched around uncomfortably in wet shoes and socks. It was a pitiful sight to see Xiao Qu looking like a wet ball of mud and shivering with the cold. If the ground outside the hut had been strewn with rice straw instead of coarse chaff, we could have used it to clean her off and then rub her dry. As it was, we had no choice but to chase her out into the sun to dry off. Even then it was the faint sunlight of winter, its warmth further diminished by a light but piercing wind.

Xiao Qu was accustomed to life in the backwaters of Henan where her mother always had a little milk to feed her. All we had to offer were leftover sweet potatoes and dry crusts of steamed bread which we soaked in hot water. There was one old fellow in our brigade who was always putting on a show of being very principled. When he saw us feeding Xiao Qu steamed bread made from white flour — even though they were only scraps that other people had left over — he gave the brigade leader a stern lecture: "Here you are feeding a dog with white flour. What do you think the villagers are eating?" We felt guilty and after that only dared to feed Xiao Qu bits of sweet potato that we did not eat ourselves. But these scraps, whether steamed bread or sweet potato, were inadequate nourishment even for a dog, and as a result Xiao Qu was thin and weak and never grew to be very large.

Once Axiang approached me looking very embarrassed and whispered in my ear, "I've got to tell you something." No sooner did she say this, than she began giggling shyly. Finally she calmed down long enough to splutter out her secret,

"It's Xiao Qu . . . did you know? . . . she's been . . . she's been stealing shit from the toilet and *eating* it!"

Axiang's revelation made me burst out laughing.

"From the fuss you're making I thought you'd been stealing it yourself!"

For a moment her expression became slightly more serious.

"But what if she keeps doing it? It's filthy."

I assured her she wouldn't find a dog in the village that did not eat excrement. When my daughter was sent down to the countryside for the first time, she shared a *kang* with a small boy who once defaecated all over the mat. As soon as she rushed to wipe up the mess with toilet paper, however, the mother came in to stop her from wasting the paper — not to mention the excrement! She then called out the door and a dog came bounding in, jumped up on the *kang* and wolfed it down in an instant. It even licked the baby's bottom so clean that there was no need for any washing or wiping. Every morning when you heard the villagers calling out in this fashion to their dogs, you knew they were being called to come and get their 'breakfast'.

It was only when I went to live in the countryside that I really discovered why pigs are universally regarded as filthy creatures. They have the same proclivities as dogs. All they think of is following their noses and without a moment's hesitation will knock over a person squatting to do their business without as much as a warning. Dogs, on the other hand, will at least wait patiently at one side and move, tail wagging, to indulge themselves only when the job is finished. During the time that we lived in the village we not only got to know the dogs but also made, so to speak, a positive contribution to their well-being.

If you think pigs and dogs are unclean, then what about vegetables? After all, what do they feed on? Probably most vegetarians have not given this question much thought.

I told Axiang that in Chinese there are two old sayings concerning people who refuse to change their ways or find it impossible to reform. One is, "Dogs will stop eating shit before you'll be able to change your ways"; the other is "You're like a dog swearing an oath in front of a toilet bowl." Xiao Qu was not a foreign dog, and she had never tasted the canned dog food that foreign dogs eat. She was not even as well off as the dogs of the other regiments. Someone told me their dogs were fed on scraps from the mess — no wonder they looked so sleek and well-fed. Only the pigs were allowed to have the scraps from our mess because they were regarded as a link in the chain of production. Xiao Qu's 'theft', therefore, was simply a matter of survival.

Whenever Mocun came over to the vegetable garden he always brought some pork skin with the hair still on it or some bones with cartilage hanging from them for Xiao Qu, who would jump around excitedly as Mocun approached. Once Mocun brought two rotten eggs someone had thrown away and tossed them over to Xiao Qu who licked and gobbled until not even a piece of shell was left. When I was tending the vegetable garden alone, Xiao Qu would keep me company waiting for Mocun. As soon as she spotted him heading south from the kiln, she would race out to meet him, running and jumping around him while barking and wagging her tail furiously. Not satisfied that this was enough to show her delight on seeing Mocun, she would also roll over a few times, jumping up and wagging her tail after each roll. Mocun had probably never had such an enthusiastic welcome in his life. Since he couldn't even take a step forward without tripping over Xiao Qu, I would have to call her to heel before the three of us could return to the vegetable fields together.

I had a colleague who never tired of telling me about his darling three-year-old grandson. Whenever the boy went to welcome his granddad home, he would jump around shouting and even roll on the ground. My colleague's face would always light up with a broad smile when he told me this. I agreed that the little boy sounded adorable, but didn't dare to compare him aloud to our dog, Xiao Qu. Still, I often thought: are dogs like people or are people like dogs? Or is it simply that babies, whether human or canine, have certain things in common?

Xiao Qu always followed after people she knew. Before our regiment moved to our barracks near the headquarters, everytime Axiang and I went back for a meal, Xiao Qu would want to follow us. She was still small and would toddle after us tripping over her own feet in the cutest way. But since we were worried that she would get too tired if she came with us, we always put her into the kennel with a brick across the front to keep her inside. One evening when we had got about halfway back to the regiment we suddenly discovered that Xiao Qu was following us. She had broken out of her kennel. It had been raining and the path was very slippery, but she ignored all of our shouts and threats, and followed us doggedly to the mat-covered structure that served as both kitchen and mess hall, falling over her own feet all the way. Everyone took a liking to her and gave her their scraps. After the feast, Xiao Qu followed the brigade leader back to the vegetable garden. That was her first big outing.

When I was sole caretaker of the vegetable garden I used to go to Mocun's mess for meals. The makeshift kennel was no longer strong enough to keep Xiao Qu in, so I would put her in the hut. Once as I was just about to reach the kiln, I turned around and spotted Xiao Qu sneaking after me at a distance. I figured she must have squeezed through one of the walls of the hut. When I called out to her to stay, she stopped dead in her tracks, but when I reached Mocun's dormitory, she appeared soon after. As soon as she caught sight of Mocun she began leaping around excitedly, much to the delight of Mocun's dog-loving colleagues, who competed with each other to feed her. Xiao Qu had got another filling meal.

At first Xiao Qu used to wait for Mocun in the garden, but later she would follow him on his return trip from the post office, though she would only go as far as the stream and then head back. One day Mocun discovered that Xiao Qu had followed him quite a distance. Worried that she was too exhausted to go any further, he carried her back to the garden where he had me hold on to her while he ran off. Of all things, Mocun arrived back at his dormitory with the mail that day only to discover Xiao Qu waiting for him at the door, jumping and barking her usual welcome. Having completed her greeting she returned to the garden to keep me company.

After our regiment moved over to headquarters, Xiao Qu lived on the leftovers from the mess that our brigade leader took back for her. It wasn't very convenient, so not long after Xiao Qu also moved to headquarters. Since she had a spot near the kitchen she never lacked things to eat, but was cut off from her old territory — the vegetable garden. I got back late and didn't know where she slept, but, I thought to myself, many people in the regiment are dog-lovers so she'll be alright. There were also a few who thought of dogs as being nothing more than pets for bourgeois ladies, so I always had to be sure to be rather cool and circumspect with Xiao Qu, had never cuddled or patted her. I don't know how she managed to find where I lived so quickly, but when I got back to the dormitory one night I was told that 'your Xiao Qu' had been around a few times looking for me. I was touched by her devotion and felt sorry I could only find old bones and things for her to gnaw on to show my gratitude. From then on she wanted to follow me to the vegetable patch every morning. I had to call her to a halt, and once even had to throw a clod of earth at her to get her to stay, but even then she just stood there watching me as I walked into the distance. One drizzly day I was sitting alone in the hut when I heard a bark outside and Xiao Qu came bounding in. She kept barking happily for a while and wagged her tail before settling down by my feet. She had found her way from headquarters right up to the garden.

To go all the way to Mocun's mess for lunch was quite a trek, and it took at least half an hour to go there, eat and get back to the hut. As I was worried about leaving the garden unattended for so long I'd often buy a meal at the regimental mess hall at the foot of 'Tiger Mountain', it being only about six or seven minutes from the garden. As Xiao Qu had invited herself that day, I bought a full serving of rice and vegetables rather than my usual half serving. Though it wasn't too far from the mess back to the garden, there was a bitter wind and I was holding my two metal bowls — one filled with rice and the other with vegetables — unprotected in my hands, so by the time I arrived everything was stone cold. I had to chew every small mouthful many times to make the food warm and soft enough to swallow. Naturally, Xiao Qu could not wait for me to finish, and jumped around expectantly, hoping to be fed. I held my rice bowl up high in one hand and spooned out some rice and some of the side dish into my own mouth and then put a bit on a piece of paper which I set down for Xiao Qu. If I hadn't done this, she would have jumped up and licked my bowl and spoon. We continued eating in this fashion until we had finished everything. I then washed up, set everything in order and took Xiao Qu back.

Far from being able to act as my guard dog, Xiao Qu usually ended up needing me to protect her. In the space of a few months she had grown from a little puppy to a full-sized bitch. In the area, there was a fierce dog called Tiger, who was kept to guard the timber and the other provisions stored on 'Tiger Mountain', as well as a sturdy grey mongrel, both of whom were interested in Xiao Qu. But she was still small, and naturally shyed from them. Whenever she came to the vegetable garden to be with me, I would have to see her back safely to the barracks, and keep those two dogs away. There was one section of the path that followed the course of the stream and I walked on top of the built-up bank while she obediently followed, hiding herself by going along the little path at the side of the stream. Only when we had crossed over the bridge and were safely on the other side did she relax.

Fortunately, both of those dogs knew me. I made a point of making friends with them. I remember one occasion when I took longer over dinner than usual and by the time I had washed up it was already pitch black outside. I had just reached the main road to the west of the garden when I was startled by the sound of barking close by. First I saw only a pair of shining eyes. Looking more carefully I could make out the large dark form of a dog, its back bent defensively as it glared back at me. It was Tiger, the most vicious animal in the cadre school. When I was still living with a family in the village, I had lost my way going home one night and slipped on the unfamiliar path. In a flash all of the dogs in the village were rushing out at me barking. I stopped and shouted 'Dog!' — the way the villagers did as none of the animals had names — and they gradually backed away. That is, all except for Tiger who kept coming towards me. I was terrified but managed to call out his name sharply, and though he did not attack me, he circled around my feet barking and sniffing menacingly for a while before losing interest and going off. After that, whenever I came across him on my way back from buying dinner I would give him something to eat. I can't remember the name of the grey dog, but he was a mate of Tiger's. Whenever I crossed their path I would call out and remember what I had been told as a child: never let a dog know you're scared. As I was very careful to avoid trouble with them I suppose they never realised how petrified I was.

After moving into the barracks at the centre of the school we all had to take turns doing guard duty at night. Each regiment had its own system. We had four two-hour shifts, the first being from ten to midnight, and the last from four till six in the morning. The first and last shifts were for the older and unhealthy members of the company, the reason being that it was less disturbing to go to bed a bit later or get up a little earlier than usual than to be woken in the middle of the night to go on duty. There was only one person on the first shift and two on the other three, as most thefts were said to take place in the early hours around three to four o'clock. No one was particularly enthusiastic about doing the first shift alone, and since I preferred going to bed late, I volunteered to do it. So putting the communal leather greatcoat over my shoulders and taking a flashlight in hand, I would start off on my rounds in the vicinity of the dormitories just after lights out at ten. I would go right up north, circle around the open field where films were shown and then return by way of the vegetable garden and pigsties. Ten minutes after lights out there was no sound of human activity to be heard anywhere. Time passed painfully slowly as I walked in the dark, but I was not always alone — sometimes Xiao Qu would come scampering up with a bark and join me on my interminable rounds.

Xiao Qu reminded me of 'Huahuar', our cat who came to meet me on my way home from Qinghua University during the 'Three-anti' movement* in the early fifties. I had always been easily scared: I didn't care whether ghosts actually existed or not, all I knew was that I was terrified of them. At night even open and well-lit places sent shivers down my spine, not to mention dim or even dark corners, and I was too scared to cross the courtyard of our house to get from one room to another.

I was cured of this irrational fear of ghosts during the 'Three-anti' movement. In our department at the university we had meetings until eleven or twelve every night, after which I would have to walk all the way to our house at the other end of the campus alone. There were a few spots along that path that gave me the heebie jeebies when I passed through them in the day or even when I was with someone at dusk. But during the 'Three-anti' movement I lost my fear. Mocun had been temporarily transferred to work in town and was living away from home, Ayuan was boarding at her school in the city, and by the time the nightly meeting was over our maid would be asleep and Huahuar was the only one to come out to fetch me home, waiting for me silently behind the trees. She would slink up with a 'meow' and grab hold of my heel in her paws. Luckily I had over-

---

* A nationwide political campaign of the early 1950's aimed against corruption, waste and bureaucracy in the Communist Party, the Government and the Army.

come my fear of the dark, otherwise she would have frightened me out of my skin. Then she would run off some distance ahead and walk back to meet me, running off again and walking back to me all the way back home, streaking away along the last stretch of the path so she could be waiting to greet me at the front door, which I'd open with my key and let us both in.

Xiao Qu was much more dependent than Huahuar, and she stayed close at my side all the time. But at night as I walked with her I thought of Huahuar and the past. We had lost her while we were moving house and we decided never to have another cat. I suppose if I had been able to keep the Buddhist injunction 'ye spend not three nights under a mulberry tree'* in mind, then I wouldn't have let myself feel such affection for a dog. But she seemed to have chosen me as her master—or perhaps it was that *I* couldn't give her up.

Once one of the people in our company rode his bike to Xinchai and Xiao Qu ran along after him all the way. This fellow was very partial to dogs and treated her to a bowl of noodles at the end of the trip, and then brought her back in the basket on the front of his bike. She was exhausted and when they got back to the company everyone thought she was dead because she didn't move or make a sound. When I returned from the vegetable garden one of them rushed up to me and said, "Your Xiao Qu is dead, come and have a look." I immediately ran with him to where Xiao Qu was lying. As soon as she heard me call her name she jumped up and starting barking and wagging her tail. Everyone cried out in relief. I had no idea that so many people cared about her.

At Chinese New Year the cooks bought a dog so we could

---

* Buddha lived as a wandering mendicant and consciously kept himself from forming any worldly attachments.

have a special meal of dog meat to celebrate, dog meat being cheaper than pork. Some peasants loved their dogs and were unwilling to sell them no matter what, while others were prepared to sell them but could not bear to butcher them. Then there were those who would accomodate the purchaser by killing the animal too. Our mess bought a dog that had already been killed. According to northern tastes you should cook the meat on a fire stoked with kindling and then eat it with finely chopped shallots after it has been simmered until the meat is nearly falling from the bones. I wonder if that's how *The Water Margin* hero Lu Zhishen did it in the old days? Anyway, our cooks made it according to Axiang's recipe of 'red cooking' it in oil and soy with lots of shallots and ginger. When I got back that evening I made a point of buying a serving of the meat to see how it had turned out, and offered it around to let my friends have a taste, too. It was very tender, but not too lean; in fact, it tasted just like a choice slice of pork. I was told that Xiao Qu refused to eat the meat, either cooked or raw. The poet said that she had carried the meat away, dug a hole and buried it. I didn't believe him and tried to talk him out of his story, but he stuck to his guns and said she really had taken the meat away in her mouth and buried it. I still think he made it all up.

The news that the whole cadre school was moving was completely unexpected. The leadership told us that all regiments that had dogs would have to leave them behind. A PLA unit was stationed at the central camp of the school just before we moved out so Axiang and I took Xiao Qu over to them, explained that we were not allowed to take her with us and asked them if they'd look after her. "Don't worry, we'll take care of her," one of the soldiers said, "lots of us here like animals." We told him that her name was "Xiao Qu", and called her a few times so they would know how to call her in the future.

Everything was pretty chaotic the day we left, so no one saw Xiao Qu. She probably went to find another dog to play with.   After we had settled down in Minggang someone in our regiment went back to the old school to take care of some unfinished business, and on their return told us that Xiao Qu would not eat and kept running around barking as though searching for someone.   Who was she looking for? Me?   Mocun?   Or some of the other people who cared for her?   Some of us regretted that we had not disobeyed orders and brought her along with us to Minggang.   But all of the dogs that had been brought to the new school were chased away in the end.

I often asked Mocun, "I wonder how Xiao Qu is now?"

"She was probably eaten by someone and is nothing more than a pile of shit now," he'd reply.

"Maybe, but she also might be a mother living off scraps and raising litters of little puppies . . . "

Misadventure
Chapter on Good Fortune

No one who was in the cadre school in Xi County will ever forget the rain — the endless drizzle that streamed down from the grey clouds that hung heavily over us, the constant wet soaking the ground through and turning everything underfoot into a muddy paste. The roads, formerly rutted with cart-wheel grooves baked sharp and hard as blades by the cruel sun, had, in the rain, turned into a treacherous swamp that made every step a hazard and even made a walking-stick useless in the struggle to keep from slipping and falling into the mud.

At first when we were still living with the villagers we had to walk some distance to the kitchen, and in the rainy weather people often straggled in so caked in mud that they looked as though they had rolled along the ground to get there. The kitchen was a flimsy structure covered in woven mats, with a similar hut for vehicles and tools next door. All of us would try and crowd into the two huts with our bowls of food. The ground was fairly dry in the centre but near the edges it was muddy and open to the wind and rain, and no matter where you finally ended up standing you would always be under a leak in the roof. After the meal we'd then have to brave the treacherous mud to slip and slide to the well to wash our bowls, and having filled up a thermos with hot water there was the walk back to the billet. Each step was fraught with danger because if you broke the thermos there was no way to replace it in the commune, and you would never be able to get one sent from Beijing that would arrive in one piece. There was nothing like Xi County in the rain to dampen the spirits.

Once, it had been raining non-stop for a few days and we had been doing political study together all morning. After lunch only administration personnel and political activists had to stay on, the rest of us were left to our own devices for the remainder of the day. Most people went back to their billets and busied themselves writing letters, mending clothing or making new clothes for the winter. I was living in the assistant brigade leader's place and though it was a small house encircled by a sea of mud like every other dwelling, it was a little neater than the rest. A solitary rectangular window had been gouged out of the mud wall of our room on the southern side of the house over which we had glued some paper to keep out the wind without shutting out the light. My bunk was in a windless but dank corner which enveloped me in a shadow so dark that I couldn't see anything around me. Aside from being a place to go back to sleep in at night, it held no attraction for me in the daytime. The only light in the room came from the faint glimmer around the papered window, and that afternoon I did not want to deprive anyone else of it. Anyway, I was in my mud-covered rain gear already and didn't really feel like making an effort to change, nor did I have anywhere to put my dripping umbrella. So with it in one hand and a walking-stick in the other I went back out into the rain.

I was always happiest when it rained in my hometown of Suzhou. The leaves on the trees in the back garden seemed to shine as they hung heavy with the jasmine rain, and the pebbles on the ground were washed clean and smooth by the water. It made me feel renewed and purified just looking outside and breathing in the moist, cool air. But the rain of Xi County was relentless and made you feel as though the muck that covered you all day had become part of your skin, and that even your bones and marrow were slowly turning into a mud paste. I picked my way through the quicksand mire out of the village, and looked at my watch. It was still early, just after two o'clock. I suddenly had an impulse to go and visit Mocun. Although I knew it was against regulations, it was hardly likely they would sound the bugle for an assembly, line us all up and do a head-count in that weather. So I decided to sneak out along the side of the kitchen and make for the main road to the west.

The fields were a patchwork of trenches that usually lay dry, but in the rain they had filled to become a network of waterways. I crossed over a bridge to find that the water in one of the trenches had spilled over and joined up with the puddle on the other side of the bridge to form a river. But since it was only a few more steps to the road, I tested the depth of the water first with one foot and then with the other, and, although there were a few places where my boot went in a little too deep, managed to make it to the other side without falling in. I then looked back to see if I was being followed and dashed over to the road, thinking to myself that I would have to find another way to get back.

It was impossible to go very fast so I picked my way carefully. My rain boots got heavier and heavier as the mud caked on them, and every so often I had to stop and scrape them with my stick. They were new boots and came up very high on the leg, but the mud was like glue, and threatened to pull them off my feet with each step. I soon lost count of how many times I nearly left a boot rooted in the mud. Little dollops of mud were constantly finding their way inside as well.

Walking on the southern side of the road, I thought the ground on the other side had more grass and would be more solid, but when I crossed over I began looking back to the southern side with longing since it now seemed to be the grassier path and I'd have had a surer footing if I had continued on that side. It was a fairly even and straight road, but just near the kiln there were a few dozen yards where the ground had given way. When we had been digging the well, Axiang and I were in charge of pushing a hand-cart loaded with everyone's food from the mess to the garden, and I remembered this spot as I had to get Axiang to ease the cart down the incline and then push it up the other side so the food and water would not spill. After all the rain we had been having, the caved-in section had filled up with water and looked like a shallow dam. There were two strips of ground running through it and I fretfully took a step on one of them only to have my foot sink deep into the ground: they were only the mud ridges of furrows made by passing vehicles. I had gone this far and though I had hit a difficult part of what was otherwise an even road I was not willing to give in and go back. I could see that there was a couple of inches between the water-line and the top of my boots so I edged my way forward. The ground was sandy and grassy in places with an occasionally firm spot, so with the help of my walking-stick I moved on and to my own surprise finally made it safely to the other side.

I should have taken a northward course from the rise on which the kiln was built, but the rivulet that usually edged its way passed the kiln and collected in a pool before being fed into the open fields was now awash with rainwater and was flowing rapidly, having formed a small island. I followed it a little way to the north but saw that it only became wider the further it went. The cluster of buildings was visible farther on the other side of the stream and I could even make out Mocun's low grey-tiled dormitory in the last row. The water was a few yards across up there and it was impossible to get through. Moreover, the wooden bridge I usually used had been washed out and lay listless, half submerged in the erratic flow of the water. A mist of grey rain had dissolved the earth and sky into one, but the stream in front of me abruptly cut the world into two again before my feet.

I gazed over at the buildings. Mocun lived in the room on the western end of the building at the back. There wasn't a soul in sight. I suddenly realised how foolish I'd look if anyone saw me. I had no choice but to turn back and try to think of another way across as I made my way back along the muddy path. The stream tapered as it moved south. It occurred to me that I might get across if I jumped over to the small island formed by the rain. The other side was a sea of mud dotted with rocks and there was no road or path, but then there were no more streams or canals to be crossed either. The bank was slippery, and cloth shoes would have given me surer footing than my rain boots. I had no idea whether the island was solid ground or just a mound of soft mud. As soon as I got close enough I poked at it with my stick. It was solid. I pushed the walking-stick in as deep as it would go and used it to steady myself as I crossed over. The rest of the way was full of potholes and craters, each step landing me in mire. My travails finally ended when I reached the entrance of Mocun's dormitory.

I pushed the door open and walked in. Mocun stared at me wide-eyed.

"What in heaven's name are you doing here?"

"I came over to see you," I said with a laugh.

He was furious that I'd broken the rules and wanted me to go back immediately. I had already made up my mind to leave when I looked at my watch and realised that it had taken me twice as long as usual to get there. I was also a little worried that the island would be washed away by the rain and I wouldn't be able to make it back to the other side. It was murky enough outside without my waiting around for it to get dark, and if I wasn't careful I'd definitely end up falling into the mud.

Someone from Mocun's regiment was heading east past the kiln to headquarters so I told him that the bridge was down. He replied that it didn't matter as there was another way, so I went along with him. Mocun put on some boots and came out with an umbrella to see us off. After we had passed the kiln I said goodbye to my companion and continued on my way eastwards. Since I was returning along the same way I'd come, as long as I wasn't too reckless or impatient I had nothing to worry about. By the time I reached the kitchen it was already dark outside and past dinnertime, but the lights were still on inside and I could hear voices. I snuck around the back like a thief and hurried off to my billet as fast as I could go without slipping in the mud.

I can't remember what I did about dinner. Perhaps I had a piece of steamed bread next to my bunk to munch on or maybe Mocun had given me something to eat before I left. Or perhaps I just went hungry. All I remember is the relief I felt at not having fallen into the river, slipped in the mud or been caught by the leadership. Moreover, none of my roommates had noticed anything out of the ordinary.

In early winter our regiment moved into the barracks we had built. The Army Propaganda Team decided to let us enjoy a proper New Year celebration so that we wouldn't get too homesick. So on New Year's eve we were given a really good meal.

Our Institute of Foreign Literature had originally belonged to the Institute of Literature, and a few women like myself had 'old men' (Mocun was my 'old man' — regardless of age, all husbands were referred to as 'so-and-so's old man') in their regiment. That night the husbands were invited over to join us for the New Year's banquet. The cooks produced an impressive array of delicious dishes: smoked fish, soy sauce chicken, red-cooked pork, curry beef and so on. There was also a tasty cold dish made from vegetables.

Mocun sat at the large rectangular table of our vegetable

brigade with the rest of us. Xiao Qu positioned herself under the table and gorged herself to bursting, wagging so much that I thought her tail would fall off.

I couldn't help thinking of the time when Mocun and I had celebrated our birthdays together in the cadre school. Our frugal banquet had consisted of nothing more than a can of red-cooked chicken. I had the day off but Mocun was on duty. On rest days we only got two meals instead of the usual three, and after breakfast I went off to see him. For some reason I didn't feel like eating much at lunch, and since I had to get back to my own regiment before Mocun's regiment had dinner I missed the main meal at our mess and had to settle for a few mouthfuls of dry steamed bread. This New Year party, however, was different: we had delicious food and good wine, and although neither of us drink, it was a pleasure to be with everyone in such a festive atmosphere, momentarily forgetting all of our cares. At the end of the meal I went out with Mocun to see him part of the way back to his barracks, talking as we walked. When we reached the bridge where the tractor had overturned he suggested I head back as we were still only halfway to his place.

Earlier on that evening there had been a heavy snowfall. When it melted, the road had turned to slush. The path leading north from the bridge had been completely covered by the snow and since it was dusk I was worried that Mocun would get lost. So I brushed aside his protests and said I'd see him all the way to his dormitory.

In the snow the path and fields all seemed to melt into one, and it was difficult to tell whether we were still on the path at all. I was careful to make a mental note of all visible landmarks so I'd be able to find my own way back: if we took a turn with a clump of large trees or smaller saplings, what shape the leaves on the trees were, just where the road banked around a corner, where the snow was the thickest and just where the irrigation channels lay — in short, generally remembering what places I would have to watch out for on my return.

The lights in Mocun's dormitory were on, and as it was getting late I decided to return immediately. A young fellow in the room offered to see me back since it was so dark. I was tempted to accept but didn't think it fair for me to drag him from the warm and convivial atmosphere of his room into the bleak and wintry evening. Mocun started worrying too but I told him that I would be fine and boasted that I travelled along that path twice a day and knew it like the back of my hand. In any case, I had a powerful flashlight.

Despite my bravado I felt a little uneasy as I usually took the way along the northern bank of the river or the north-west path on the south bank. Mocun didn't realize that in the thirty minutes since we had arrived night had come on and the path we had come along was unrecognizable. We had found his barracks fairly easily because we could see the lights from the buildings from a distance, but going back in the dark was another matter altogether. I was adamant and said I did not need anyone to see me back, and he didn't force the issue. He saw me out to the edge of the darkness and I told him to go back inside.

My boast that I preferred walking in the dark was really put to the test. First I calmly took my bearings. People say that women have no sense of direction, and I remember reading somewhere that women and hens lose their way outdoors. This may well be an ungrounded slight against women, but I am always losing my way, as the saying goes, "Wanting to go to the south of the city (she) strides confidently to the north." Although Mocun can never remember the exact way anywhere, I entirely rely on him for steering us in the right direction. So I stood there, oriented myself and set my course: I would first set off in a southwesterly direction after which I would veer off and go through a small forest, and after getting onto the road next to the forest I would head due west until I reached a small clump of trees, and turning south I should end up at the bridge, my usual path and the familiar homestretch.

No sooner had I stepped out of the light of the building than I found myself in a dark abyss. There was not a star visible in the looming sky, and the ground was an unbroken, formless sheet of white. I could see no trees, no road, and when I turned on my flashlight no more than a few unfamiliar tree trunks around me were visible. I closed my eyes for a moment so that I could get used to the dark and when I opened them and had a careful look around there was little more than the distant darkness and the snow. The winding path we had walked along through the trees with the aid of the light from the buildings was completely indiscernable now that the faint light of dusk had gone. I felt like turning right around and asking someone to take me back, but realized that since everything was covered in snow, an extra pair of eyes probably would not be much help. Moreover, whoever saw me back would still have to return alone, so I decided that it was best to stick to my original resolve.

I looked around with renewed determination and making a rough guess where southeast was I stepped out into the darkness. I knew that if I set my course too far to the west then I wouldn't be able to get out of the wood, so I edged slightly to the south. Under the weight of my boots the white ground turned to mud, but as the snow had covered scattered straw, lengths of discarded hemp rope and leaves, it wasn't too slippery. I moved steadily south, and when my way was blocked by trees I diverted to the west. When I turned around to see how far I'd got I discovered that the lights were no longer to be seen: I had lost my sole point of reference. A moment later I seemed to be treading on nothingness and found myself at the bottom of a ditch. The fall gave me a bad shock but also jolted my memory: there was a wide and deep ditch running along the side of the road next to the wood — that was the ditch I had fallen into! I was both happy and relieved, and quickly turning on my flashlight I found a way out of the ditch and onto the road.

There was no snow on the main road so I grew more confident, though now I began worrying about the southern turnoff. If I kept on walking I knew I would end up in the neighbouring village beyond headquarters.   Trees were growing evenly spaced on either side of the road, but all I could make out were the lower part of the tree trunks. The trees that I had been so careful to remember on the trip to Mocun's seemed to have disappeared without a trace. Or was it that I had just lost my way and those memorized forms stood unchanged along some other part of the road? If that was the case then I wouldn't be able to find the bridge where the tractor had turned over. It would be better to turn off a little early than walk past the spot and end up in some fields where I might wander around lost all night. I turned south at the next clump of trees.

Moments after leaving the road I was lost again. A little further on I found myself in a patch of uncut millet stalks. I kept walking straight, reckoning that as long as I kept moving south I would be able to find the river and then could follow it to the bridge.

I'd heard stories about bad men lurking in fields late at night and I tried to keep as quiet as possible, worried that if I made too much noise I might also attract the attention of a wild dog. I steered a careful course through the field without rustling the dry stalks. It was muddy, but not slippery. I concentrated all of my senses on my forward progress. The flashlight — the only piece of equipment available to me — remained unused. I finally came to a large embankment: it was the river! But in the snow and dark everything seemed unfamiliar, and since both sides of the river had similar embankments I couldn't tell whether I was on the western or eastern side of the stone bridge. If I was already on the western side of the bridge then I would have to keep going until I reached the kiln, then go past it to the other side of headquarters before I could cross over and walk eastwards back to my billet. I had heard that someone in the school had hung himself in the kiln recently.   Luckily I wasn't the faint-hearted person I was in the past or I would have just wandered around on the river bank too scared to go on in case I met up with the ghosts of the drowned tractor driver or the hanged man. I decided that I had turned off too soon and was still to the east of the bridge, so I started walking west. It wasn't long before I found the bridge. After crossing over I still had a long way to go, but the route was familiar and I got back in no time at all.

"You're back?" My roommates asked merrily as though I had just taken a short after-dinner stroll. In the comforting light of the room it was hard to imagine the forbidding darkness outside.

In the early spring of 1971 our Academy of Studies cadre school was ordered to move from Xi County to join up with divisional headquarters in Minggang. It was stated that our main duty was no longer participation in physical labour, but 'study' — the study of class struggle. Those of us who were still unclear about the real aims of the Academy of Studies were finally enlightened that we were supposed to be the Academy of 'Political' Study.

Even something as innocent as going to see a film became a form of political study and was just like being at school — no one was allowed to be absent. As Mocun had poor eyesight and could not even see the screen he was given 'cinematic immunity'.

On the evenings when films were shown we would all have to line up after dinner and march off to the open-air 'theatre', everyone taking their own folding stool. Each regiment had an appointed spot and we would plant our stools in position and sit in uniform rows. Even if it had been raining we'd have to put our stools down on our assigned places and sit down. If it was still raining we'd take along raincoats — no cancellations due to inclement weather for us. In the summer there would be hordes of mosquitoes to contend with. But there was one saving grace about this part of our 'education' — there were no examinations, so when I grew tired I could shut my eyes and have a rest. As there was only a very limited number of films that could be shown you could afford to doze off for a while without worrying about missing anything. There would always be ample opportunity to see the film a few more times in the future. There were thirty people in each dormitory and after each showing there would be endless discussion about the film. I always listened on in silence, not wishing to reveal my ignorance.

One time after a film I followed a group back to the barracks. Though I was awake I kept my eyes on the ground and followed, half asleep in my own dream-world. The people I was with split up and I went along with one group until I realized that I was in the corridor of an unfamiliar dormitory. I rushed back outside and discovered that I'd been walking with another regiment, and that the last stragglers were hurrying off to their own buildings. I had no idea where I was and none of the people I asked knew how I could get back to my regiment. They were all interested in getting back to their own rooms and didn't have any time for me. I suddenly felt as though I had unwittingly drifted into a foreign land, surrounded as I was by strange and unfamiliar people.

Outside I looked up at the sky, and although I couldn't tell my way by the position of the stars, I did know that the few stars I was familiar with were in the wrong place and that I was a long way from my dormitory. The camp covered a huge area and the barracks were locked in a cobweb of winding paths. If I wandered off without knowing where I was going and was caught in a maze of unfamiliar buildings when lights out was called then it would be very difficult to find my way back. There was only one solution: to get onto the brick road that ran along the southern side of the barracks, and from there it would be easy to find my way back. The open-air cinema was just near the road, and I was sure the dormitories I had come to were not too far from the cinema. Since most of the buildings faced south and the north star was behind them, all I had to do was walk south away from the buildings and I would eventually come across the road. Even if this was the long way of going about it, at least I could be sure I wouldn't get any more lost.

My main worry was making it back before lights out. I followed the crooked lanes south and went through the vegetable garden, hoping that this would be the fastest way. The garden in the new school was quite different from our old vegetable patch: the earth was fertile and full of vegetables. It was also just one big field, not divided into sections. They had dug deep pits for fertilizer at the end of every few rows. Not long ago a tall young man in our regiment had fallen into one of these pits on the way back from watching a film. He managed to crawl out and get back to the 'water room' — our name for the washroom — in our dormitory and spent hours washing himself clean with cold water before slipping back into his room unnoticed. I was sure that if I fell into one of the pits I would sink like a rock, and even if I did manage to hang on to one of the sides and call for help there would be no one around to hear me. The only consolation in such an ignominious end was that I wouldn't have to go back to the dormitory and freeze myself to death washing in the cold water.

Since I always went out with a group of other people at night I hadn't taken the trouble to change the batteries in my flashlight, and the light it threw out was barely enough to make out that there were vegetables all around me, and not what kind they were. I did an imitation of Piggy crossing the ice*: instead of carrying a pole I put my stool on my

---

* Piggy (Zhu Bajie) is one of the main characters in *Journey to the West*, also known as *Monkey*, a classical Chinese novel about the monk Xuan Zhuang's journey to India to obtain Buddhist sutras. Piggy is one of the members of the little troupe and shares in its adventures, using his hoe to ward off the enemy and save himself from tight situations.

shoulder so that if I fell into one of the pits I'd at least have something to hang on to. Such precautions weren't really necessary, as no one would have come to my aid and I would have drowned in the end anyway. I forced myself not to think too much about what could happen, and armed with stool and flashlight I walked on ahead, kicking the vegetable leaves with each step to make sure they weren't hiding a fertilizer pit. It was very slow going and I felt as though I were feeling my way blindly towards the edge of a cliff. I finally got out of the vegetable patch, crossed an irrigation channel and walked straight into yet another vegetable patch. It was a nightmare, and I walked on and on for what seemed like ages with no idea of just where I was going.

Fortunately, I had been heading in the right direction, and having cleared the second vegetable patch I crossed a path covered in coal cinder and finally reached the paved road after walking through a stretch of ground covered with wild grass and rocks. I broke out into a jog and then slowed down to a walk, took a turn to the north and ran all the way back to my dormitory. The lights were still on and the last group was just returning from the toilets. I calculated that I had only been in the vegetable fields for about twenty minutes. Thankfully I hadn't gone the wrong way and it must have seemed that I was just returning from the toilet — no one would have believed that I had walked off with the wrong group after the film. I wonder when they would have found me if I really had fallen into one of the pits? As I lay down on my hard little bunk I felt indescribably safe and peaceful.

A colleague a few years younger than me had a brain haemorrhage while squatting on his stool watching a film one night after dinner. He didn't move when everyone else got up to go. He was paralysed and was rushed to the clinic but died soon after. Following this incident the older 'students' in the school were given permission to be absent from film 'classes'. I often wondered if I had called out for help in front of that unfamiliar dormitory whether the older people in the school would have been given this reprieve a little sooner. But I suppose my shouts of distress would not have been 'tragic' enough to deserve serious attention, and would have been turned into a negative example of a typically woolly intellectual.

These three misadventures brought me face to face with what I thought was danger, though in fact nothing eventually happened. Only if something very unfortunate had occurred would the danger have been real.

Rumours
Chapter on Self-deception

The cat in the house where I was living in Yang Village once played a nasty trick on me. A single oil-lamp hung near the door of our room. My bed was in the corner, hidden in the shadows. One evening when I came back with my roommates from brushing my teeth and washing up, I could make out two dark objects on my bed. Luckily, I didn't put out a reckless hand to feel what it was because when I switched on my flashlight and shone it in that direction I discovered a dead mouse with its intestines torn out and lying beside it.

No one was willing to touch it, and only after some time did I nervously move my quilt and pillow to one side, lift up the sheet with the help of one of my roommates and carry it outside, dumping the grisly remains onto the compost heap. Next morning at the crack of dawn I went out to wash the sheet. I washed and dried it many times, but the pink blood stain looked like it would never go away.

When I saw Mocun I told him about this gruesome episode and explained that the cat must have been making me a special 'present' of its catch. He tried to cheer me up with some impromptu augury.

"This is a very auspicious omen. The word 'mouse' (*shu*) indicates this place (*chu*); and for a disemboweled mouse to be put on your bed with its entrails next to it symbolises parting. It may well mean that you'll be leaving here."

I couldn't help laughing: no matter what mystical significance he read into it, I knew full well that I was not going anywhere. I imitated the strident tones of the big-character posters and cried, "This has revealed the origin of your corrupt ideology! Abandon your vain hopes of escape!" Despite his efforts to console me, we both knew that 'freedom is the recognition of necessity.' The way out was blocked, and no amount of force would be able to clear it.

Towards the end of that year Mocun came into the garden one day and told me a piece of completely unexpected news. As a result of helping the people at the post office read rare and difficult characters in place names on articles of mail, he was often treated to a cup of tea when he made his daily visit — not the boiled water that the locals usually called 'tea', but the real thing made from tea leaves. That day his friend in the post office had told him that they'd received a telegram from Beijing for the cadre school, directing them to send a group of 'old, weak, ill and disabled' cadres back to the capital. Mocun's name was, he said, on the list.

I was delighted. If Mocun could go back to Beijing and be together with Ayuan, I would have no qualms about staying on alone. I would automatically be given leave once a year to visit them. It was only because we were both in the same county and the same cadre school, even though we lived apart, that we were not eligible to apply for leave hitherto.

A few days later Mocun departed from his usual routine and came over to see me before going back to his regiment with the mail. They'd received the official list of people who could go back and he had heard that he was on it. I was already thinking about how I would get him packed up and ready to go. All I needed to know was the date fixed for their departure. A few more days passed and Mocun came to see me again, this time with a very glum expression on his face.

"Have they made the announcement?" I asked anxiously.

They had: he was not on the list. He told me the names of all the people who would be going and my heart sank. If the rumour had not been false in the first place our hopes would not have been raised so high, and the disappointment and frustration we now felt would not have been so great.

I walked back over to the stream with him and then returned to the hut and watched him walk away with his head lowered dejectedly. Was Mocun younger or healthier than any of those who'd been given permission to leave? I recited Han Yu's poem 'To Magistrate Zhang on the Night of the 5th Day of the 8th Month'* out loud and sunk into deep thought.

I couldn't help feeling it must have been due to the 'black evidence' that was in his file, an allegation we would have never known existed if it was not for the 'Great Proletarian Cultural Revolution'. Someone had put up a wall-poster accusing Mocun of having slighted the writings of the Great Leader. Anyone who read the poster and knew Mocun was quick to point out that if Mocun had actually said such a thing he would have done it in wittier fashion. The language was not his style at all. Someone tipped me off about it and when I read it for myself I was furious. I said that when you make something up about a person it is usual to base it on some shred of truth, not simply indulge in malicious and unfounded flights of fancy.

When we were released from our respective 'cowsheds' and allowed to return home that day the first thing I did was to tell Mocun about the poster. We then sat down together and wrote a small-character poster suggesting why the accusations were unfounded and requesting that an investigation be made. After a hurried dinner we went off to the Academy and stuck our poster up below the original

---

* Han Yu talks of the frustration of an official banished to the southern wilds of China and who is excluded from an imperial pardon due to the calumny of others. All that is left, he sighs, is a cup of wine and forgetfulness.

one. I was 'struggled' the next day for my efforts. Later we did at least find out that someone had accused Mocun of making the statements that were in the poster. This 'testimony' had obviously been put into Mocun's file without ever being verified, and when an investigation was made that same person denied all knowledge of the accusations.

I have no doubt at all that the Red Guards were very thorough in their inquiries, and they did not manage to find any proof that Mocun had said anything wrong. Just before we were shipped off to the cadre school the Army Propaganda Team officially stated that they were taking the accusation extremely seriously, and despite the fact that there was no evidence to confirm their suspicions they were convinced that there must have been some wrongdoing for such an allegation to be made. Mocun was ordered to make a lengthy self-criticism. He had no choice but to produce a vague 'confession'. Every time I think of the episode, I still get angry.

The following day when Mocun came to the vegetable garden I told him that the old accusation had to be the cause of all the trouble. He said I was being silly, and that we shouldn't waste our time worrying about something we had no control over. I had to admit that he was right. It was folly to try and fathom such machinations in the first place, and to be obsessive about it would only make life more uncomfortable than it need be.

On the morning that the group returning to Beijing left, we all rushed out to the parade ground by the road to see them off. To see others going home when you must stay on yourself is very disquieting. My eyes followed the trucks longingly as they rolled away full of the 'graduates' of the school and their luggage. I was shaken out of my reverie by a friend tugging at my arm. We walked back to the dormitory together. She let out a heavy sigh and was about to say something but then swallowed the words. We walked to our own rooms silently.

The old, weak, infirm and disabled had all been sent back to Beijing, so the rest of us who had been left knew we would have to resign ourselves to the fact that we were in the cadre school for the rest of our lives. As I was walking to the vegetable garden it suddenly occurred to me: if Mocun really had gone would I have ever been able to recapture that feeling of belonging, of being part of that 'us' again? I knew that although I was still physically in the cadre school my attitude had changed. I no longer felt completely committed to 'us'.

My mind wandered back to the days just before Liberation when so many people were fleeing overseas. Why hadn't we taken one of the many offers and left as well? Was it because we were ideologically progressive or had a 'high level of consciousness'? Mocun often quoted Liu Yong's poem in reply, 'Though I grow thin from pining, regret does never come. Giving all for her though form and colour may fade.'* The simple fact was that we couldn't abandon our homeland, discard 'her' — the only place in the world where we could ever be part of that 'us'. Even though there are hundreds of millions of Chinese, members of the 'us' who we don't know, we are all still part of one entity. We feel as one, breathe as one, all undeniable, inseparable parts of China. I felt ashamed that I had believed the rumours and had hoped that Mocun would be going back to Beijing to live with Ayuan in safety. It was selfish of me to think only of my own family without any regard for others. In the end, that's what it all had come to: despite the endless campaigns and injunctions to reform my thinking, I was worse than I was before.

When Mocun passed the garden I pointed to the hut.

---

* These are the last two lines of a love poem by the Song dynasty poet Liu Yong.

"If we had a little hut like this one we could settle down here, couldn't we?"

He thought it over for a moment and replied dolefully,

"We don't have any books."

He was right. We could do without every other type of material comfort, but without books, life would be impossible. All he had brought with him were dictionaries, notebooks and stone rubbings.

"Have you ever regretted that we stayed in China?" I asked.

"If we could do it all again I wouldn't want to change a thing."

Mocun always made decisions quickly, as though he never gave matters much thought. But once he had made up his mind, he didn't think twice about it, nor did he try to change things. I, however, couldn't help considering things from every possible angle, although we usually arrived at the same conclusions. Since we had made our decision to stay with our eyes open, aware of the consequences, we did not look back with any regrets for what might have been.

Following the move to Minggang Mocun and I were living in barracks that were only about six minutes walking distance from each other. All of the buildings were single storey whitewashed structures with tiled roofs and glass windows. The food was better than in the canteen of the Academy in Beijing. The toilets were no longer a hole in the ground surrounded by reed walls which you had to line up to go to. We also had more room, and were able to take out the reference books and notebooks we had bought in our trunks to read. Ayuan sent us regular food packages along with a constant supply of foreign language journals and digests. All of the books being passed around were worth rereading so we never lacked for material. The setting of the new cadre school had a serene beauty about it, and there were many spots where you could go and enjoy nature.

My walks with Mocun at dusk were far more pleasant than our daily rendezvous in the vegetable garden. We no longer had to do any physical work, nor did we have to use our brains. Perhaps it was because we were being fed and paid for doing nothing that we felt so dejected. At the same time, when we saw all of the young people crowding themselves into political meetings and making speeches, we felt profoundly ill at ease.

We had been sent to cadre school to work and had nothing to do, but it was forbidden to leave. The nearest train station was only an hour away by foot, but you needed to have a special certificate stamped by the Propaganda Team to buy a ticket. Once we asked for a furlough from our respective leaders to go and see the doctor in Xinyang city as Mocun had a toothache and I was having trouble with my eyes. It turned out when we finally got there that the dentist had invented a 'massage method' for extracting teeth, wrenching out the infected tooth after doing a bit of massaging in place of the usual anaesthetic. All of the patients had run off rather than submit themselves to this revolutionary new method. Mocun and I took advantage of the confusion and slipped away to see the local sights, or sight rather, the name of which I've forgotten. It was nothing more than an unimpressive hillock and a pond that was half-dried out spanned by a crumbling old bridge. In a col there were a few plots of Chinese medicinal herbs. It wasn't much of a place for sightseeing but we were as happy as a couple of children who had skipped school.

I made a return trip to Xinyang to learn that my tear ducts were damaged, and that I'd have to go to Beijing for treatment. The doctor informed the Propaganda Team but nothing would move them: permission was simply not forthcoming. In the end I had to ask for leave of absence, and I still had to get a certificate from the Academy before I was allowed to register at the hospital. All of these vexing barriers were thrown up to dissuade people from going back to Beijing on sick-leave and then refusing to return to the cadre school.

You just had to hope you wouldn't get seriously ill while you were in the school. After I'd undergone treatment for my eyes in the capital I returned to Henan with Ayuan so she could see her father. We were sure that Mocun would be waiting for us at the station in Minggang, but when he didn't appear we went to the school by ourselves, thinking that he was probably back at the station waiting for us somewhere. It was not until we were a few minutes from his dormitory that someone told us that he'd had a bad attack of asthma and was running a high fever.

The girl in the clinic did not have enough training or experience even to qualify as a barefoot doctor, and she frankly adn.itted that Mocun was the first patient she had ever given an intravenous injection to. She had been sweating nervously when she had done it and had completely forgotten to take off the band she had put on his arm to stop the blood circulation. Despite all of this his condition had begun to improve after the second injection and by the time we arrived his temperature was nearly back to normal. The nurse pointed at herself, cocked her head and told Mocun, "Mr Qian, do you realize that I saved you?" And she was right. If she had been too scared or simply unwilling to give him those two injections, he would have had to be taken elsewhere for treatment and very possibly ended up the worse for it.

We didn't feel so worried about Ayuan after she came to visit us. We had no more to do than sit around all day in sated repose, yet all the same everyone felt a lurking sense of anxiety. Following the report of Lin Biao's 'nose dive'*, the struggle against 'May 16th Elements' in the cadre school foundered. We heard that the people who had gone back to Beijing still spent all their time at political meetings.

---

* This refers to Lin Biao's death in a plane crash in Mongolia on September 13, 1971, during his escape from China after an unsuccessful attempt to assassinate Mao Zedong.

People say that all things come to those who wait, yet that waiting and hoping itself takes something out of the happiness you should feel when your hopes are realized. In March 1971 another group of old, weak, ill and disabled cadres was given permission to return to Beijing. This time both of our names were on the list. Naturally I was looking forward to going home, but I only wished we could all be going together. Since they were sending a second group back, however, presumably there would be a third and a fourth . . . it was clear that everyone would be allowed to leave sooner or later. I was secretly thrilled that we were going back when we were. Our colleagues shared our happiness and gave us a farewell meal. The stoves in the dormitories used for heating still hadn't been taken down for the summer so we used them to cook. I lost count of all of the meals of soup dumplings we were given by friends and we even had a meal of won-ton dumplings made with herbs that we'd picked ourselves. Everyone knew that they were no more than temporary residents this time and the atmosphere was far more relaxed and lighthearted than it had been when we had all seen the first group off a year earlier. I still felt a twinge of guilt as I looked around at those who wouldn't be going back with us, yet, all that aside, I can't deny that I was ecstatic at the thought of leaving. It was clear to me that despite ten years of ideological reform and two years in a cadre school I still hadn't managed to get rid of my own selfishness, nor did I achieve the personal transformation that others had sought after so diligently. I was the same person I always had been.

It's been eight years since we came back to Beijing, and all of the little details and personal concerns of those days are still fresh in my mind. Those years provided me with a rare and unforgettable experience, and these six chapters are my record of them.

A Cadre School Life: Six Chapters

By Yang Jiang
Translated by Geremie Barmé
With the assistance of Bennett Lee

Within a few years following Mao Zedong's "May
7 Directive" of 1966, over twenty million people,
virtually all of China's professional and university-
trained population, were "sent down" to cadre
schools for "re-education". Yang Jiang, a professor
emeritus of English, and her husband Qian Zhongshu,
a respected writer and scholar, were two of the
intellectuals "sent down". In this little book, Yang
Jiang records her life in the cadre school lucidly,
attempting neither to praise nor condemn, with no
desire to theorize or declaim. Instead of detailing
the words and deeds of others, she simply chronicles
the lives of herself and her husband. The result, as
one of China's foremost critics comments, is a book
that "pervades one with a sense of sorrow and loss;
we lament as she does but do not feel dejected,
we sense her indignation at being wronged but find
in this no hate or reproach. Every word is eloquent
in its sincerity and truthfulness."

JOINT PUBLICATIONS
Modern Chinese Literature
ISBN 962.04.0222.7
HK$ 15.00

Cover design by Ya